Loom Knitting Dictionary

Add excitement to your loom knitting with pretty pattern stitches that you can substitute for plain stitches in your favorite projects. Use them to make hats, scarves, bags, afghans, and more.

CONTENTS

Meet Kathy Norris	3
Getting Started	4
Knit and Purl Stitches	6
Twisted Stitches	20
Rib Patterns	32
Color Patterns	40
Lace Patterns	64
Cables	78
General Instructions	91

LEISURE ARTS, INC.
Maumelle, Arkansas

EDITORIAL STAFF

Vice President of Product Development and Publications: Pam Stebbins
Production Director: Tona Jolly
Art Director: Marcus Boyce
Technical Writer/Editor: Cathy Hardy
Technical Editors: Linda A. Daley, Sarah J. Green, and Lois J. Long
Editorial Writer: Susan Frantz Wiles
Graphic Arts Manager: Lora Puls
Graphic Artist: Cailen Cochran
Photography Technical Manager: Stephanie Johnson
Prepress Technician: Janie Marie Wright
Contributing Photographer: Ken West

BUSINESS STAFF

President and Chief Executive Officer: Fred F. Pruss
Senior Vice President of Operations: Jim Dittrich
Vice President of Retail Sales: Martha Adams
Chief Financial Officer: Tiffany P. Childers
Controller: Teresa Eby
Information Technology Director: Brian Roden
Director of E-Commerce: Mark Hawkins
Manager of E-Commerce: Robert Young

Copyright © 2016 by Leisure Arts, Inc., 104 Champs Blvd., STE 100, Maumelle, AR 72113-6738, www.leisurearts.com. All rights reserved. This publication is protected under federal copyright laws. Reproduction or distribution of this publication or any other Leisure Arts publication, including publications which are out of print, is prohibited unless specifically authorized. This includes, but is not limited to, any form of reproduction or distribution on or through the Internet, including posting, scanning, or e-mail transmission.

We have made every effort to ensure that these instructions are accurate and complete. We cannot, however, be responsible for human error, typographical mistakes, or variations in individual work.

Library of Congress Control Number: 2016939858

ISBN-13/EAN: 978-1-4647-4619-3
UPC: 0-28906-75566-4

2 www.leisurearts.com

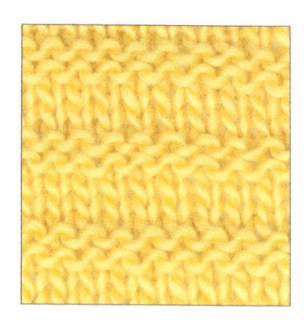

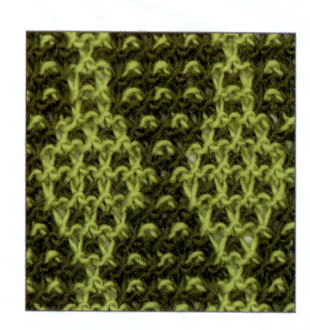

Meet Kathy Norris

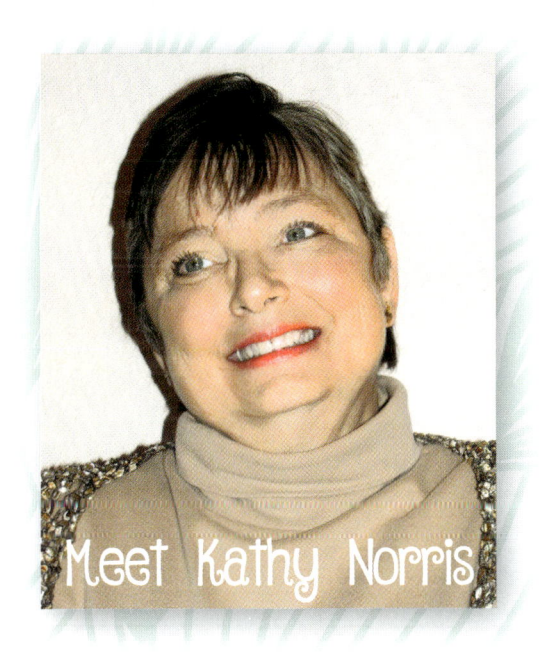

Like most people, Kathy Norris learned to knit in the traditional style, using knitting needles. She discovered loom knitting at the craft supply store where she worked in Southern California. She says, "They handed me a knitting loom and told me to figure it out. So I taught myself how to use it."

Kathy used her first loom knitting designs to teach others the fun new skill. In 2005, she began publishing her patterns. "I was attracted to loom knitting because, as a designer, you have to find a new way to work with the geometry of knitting. Once you have the loom knitting basics down, you can start experimenting to make the loom do what you want."

Leisure Arts books and ebooks featuring Kathy's designs are *More Knitting Wheel Fashions* (#4411), *I Can't Believe I'm Loom Knitting* (#5250), *Big Book of Loom Knitting* (#5604), *Loom Knitting for Mommy and Me* (#5942), *Loom Knit Dishcloths* (#6369), *Big Book of Loom Knit Cowls* (#6611), *Loom Knit Baby Wraps* (#6667), and *Loom Knit Hats and Scarves* (#75471). Learn more at KathyNorrisDesigns.com.

GETTING STARTED

This book is divided into six pattern stitch sections. Additional information is given at the beginning of each section. We've included knit and purl stitches, twisted stitches, rib patterns, color patterns, lace patterns, and cables.

KNITTING LOOM GAUGE

The gauge of your knitting is partially affected by the spacing of the pegs. The distance is measured from the center of one peg to the center of the next peg. There are many choices of knitting looms on the market. Which loom you use depends on the yarn weight you want to use.

Stitch gauge and loom size are not given for any of the pattern stitches in this book, allowing you the flexibility to choose what meets your needs.

The following chart is a guide to looms and weights of yarn that can be used.

Loom gauge	Peg Spacing	Yarn - single strand	Yarn - double strand
Regular	½" to 9/16"	#3 & #4	#2
Large	5/16" to 11/16"	#4 & #5	#3 & #4
Extra Large	¾" to 15/16"	#5 & #6	#4

MULTIPLES

The multiple indicates the number of pegs required to form one full repeat of each pattern stitch. The multiple plus the number of pegs needed to work the pattern is given with all pattern stitches; this information is invaluable when using the patterns for projects.

An example is the Swedish Block pattern on page 11, which uses a multiple of 6 + 2 pegs if working the pattern as a flat piece. You need to cast on any number of pegs that is divisible by 6, such as 6, 12, 18, etc. Then cast on an additional 2 pegs. Note that the "plus" number is added only once.

KNIT & PURL STITCHES

■□□□ BEGINNER

Many patterns can be formed by using simple combinations of knit and purl stitches. This section uses the true knit stitch. The e-wrap knit stitch is used in the twisted stitches section.

The true knit stitch tends to produce a tighter stitch than the e-wrap knit stitch. The gauge of the knit stitch is controlled by adjusting how loosely the yarn wraps around the pegs.

8

9

9

10

11

11
12
13
14
14
8
15
16
17
18

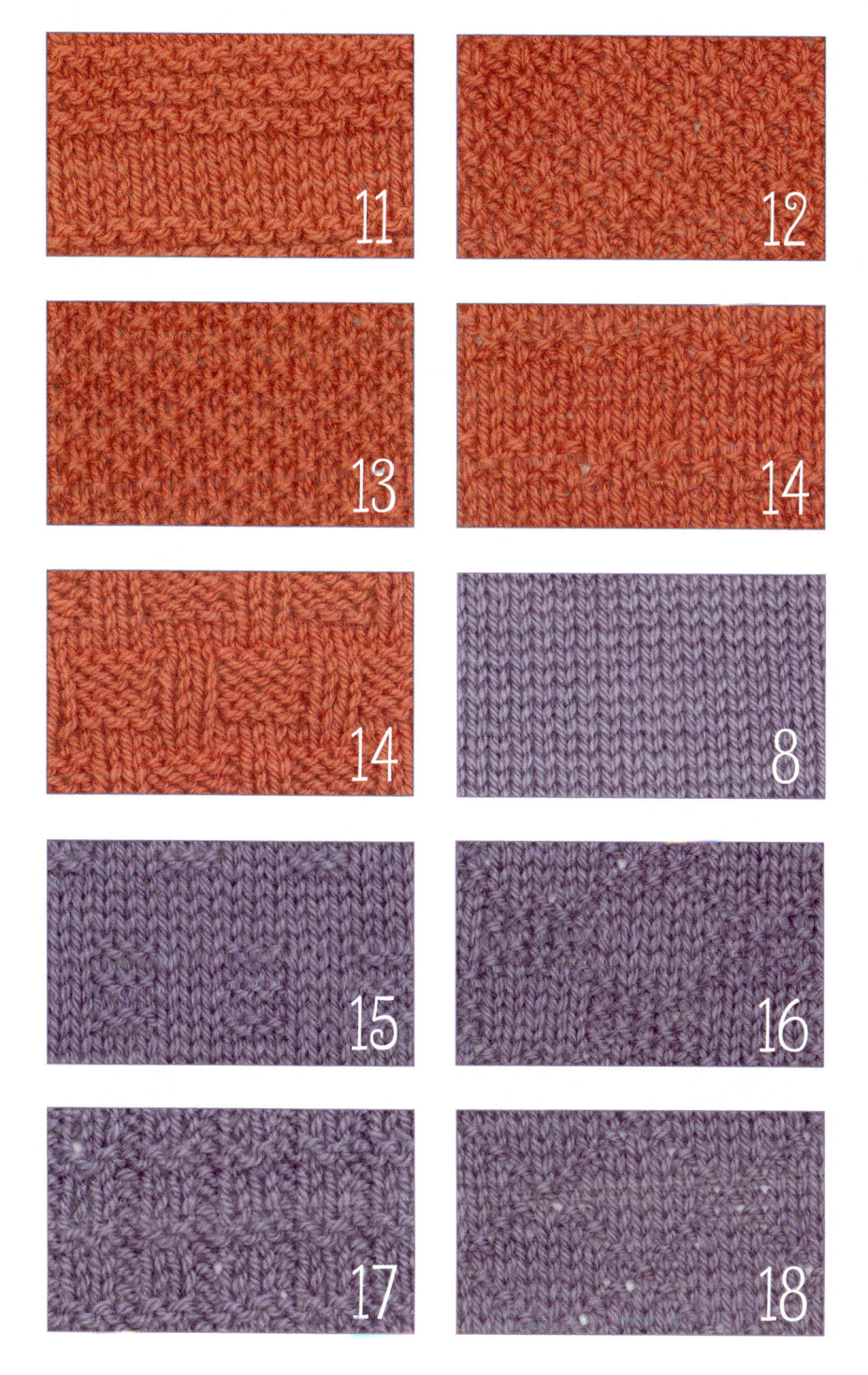

Stockinette Stitch

Multiple: any number of pegs

Worked Flat and Circular
Knit every row/rnd.

The reverse side of this stitch is called Reverse Stockinette Stitch. Purl every row/rnd for Reverse Stockinette Stitch to face you as you work.

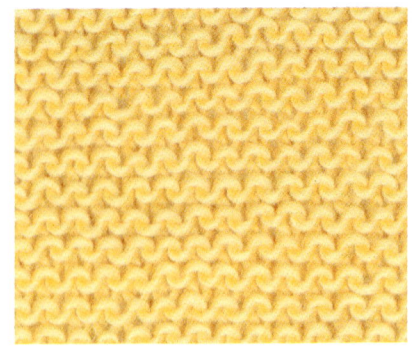

Garter Stitch

Multiple: any number of pegs

Worked Flat and Circular
Row/Rnd 1: Knit across.

Row/Rnd 2: Purl across.

Repeat Rows/Rnds 1 and 2 for pattern.

Garter Stitch is a reversible fabric that looks the same on both sides.

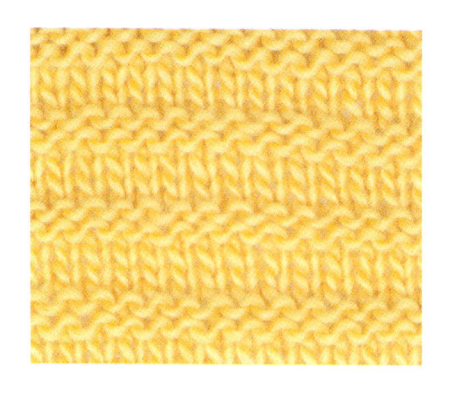

Welting Stitch

Multiple: any number of pegs

Worked Flat and Circular
Rows/Rnds 1 and 2: Purl across.

Rows/Rnds 3-5: Knit across.

Repeat Rows/Rnds 1-5 for pattern.

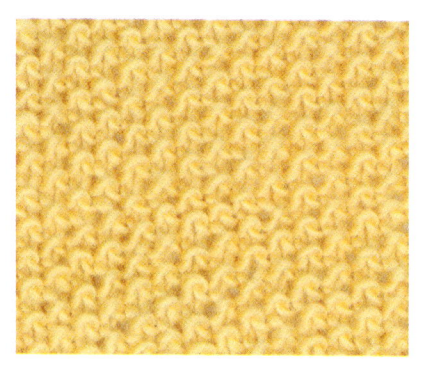

Seed Stitch

Multiple: any even number of pegs

Worked Flat
Row 1: (K1, P1) across.

Repeat Row 1 for pattern.

Worked Circular
Rnd 1: (K1, P1) around.

Rnd 2: (P1, K1) around.

Repeat Rnds 1 and 2 for pattern.

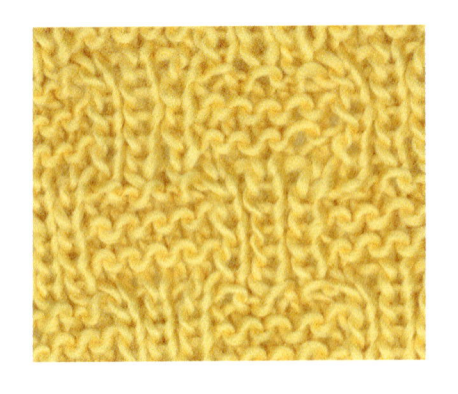

Garter & Rib Check

Multiple: 10 pegs (worked on at least 20 pegs)

Worked Flat

Row 1: (K1, P1) twice, ★ K7, P1, K1, P1; repeat from ★ across to last 6 pegs, K6.

Row 2: ★ P5, K1, (P1, K1) twice; repeat from ★ across.

Rows 3-6: Repeat Rows 1 and 2 twice.

Row 7: K6, P1, K1, P1, ★ K7, P1, K1, P1; repeat from ★ across to last peg, K1.

Row 8: ★ K1, (P1, K1) twice, P5; repeat from ★ across.

Rows 9-12: Repeat Rows 7 and 8 twice.

Repeat Rows 1-12 for pattern.

Worked Circular

Rnd 1: K6, P1, K1, P1, ★ K7, P1, K1, P1; repeat from ★ around to last peg, K1.

Rnd 2: ★ P5, K1, (P1, K1) twice; repeat from ★ around.

Rnds 3-6: Repeat Rnds 1 and 2 twice.

Rnd 7: (K1, P1) twice, ★ K7, P1, K1, P1; repeat from ★ around to last 6 pegs, K6.

Rnd 8: ★ K1, (P1, K1) twice, P5; repeat from ★ around.

Rnds 9-12: Repeat Rnds 7 and 8 twice.

Repeat Rnds 1-12 for pattern.

Swedish Block

Multiples: 6 + 2 pegs for flat and 6 pegs for circular

Worked Flat

Rows 1 and 2: K2, (P4, K2) across.

Rows 3-8: P2, (K4, P2) across.

Repeat Rows 1-8 for pattern.

Worked Circular

Rnds 1 and 2: (K2, P4) around.

Rnds 3-8: (P2, K4) around.

Repeat Rnds 1-8 for pattern.

Garter Stitch Ridges

Multiple: any number of pegs

Worked Flat and Circular

Rows/Rnds 1-5: Knit across.

Row/Rnd 6: Purl across.

Row/Rnd 7: Knit across.

Rows/Rnds 8-10: Repeat Rows/Rnds 6 and 7 once, then repeat Row/Rnd 6 once more.

Repeat Rows/Rnds 1-10 for pattern.

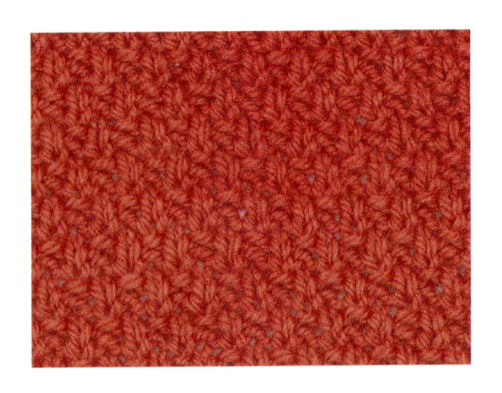

Moss Stitch

Multiple: any even number of pegs

Worked Flat

Row 1: (K1, P1) across.

Rows 2 and 3: (P1, K1) across.

Rows 4 and 5: (K1, P1) across.

Repeat Rows 2-5 for pattern.

Worked Circular

Rnds 1 and 2: (P1, K1) around.

Rnds 3 and 4: (K1, P1) around.

Repeat Rnds 1-4 for pattern.

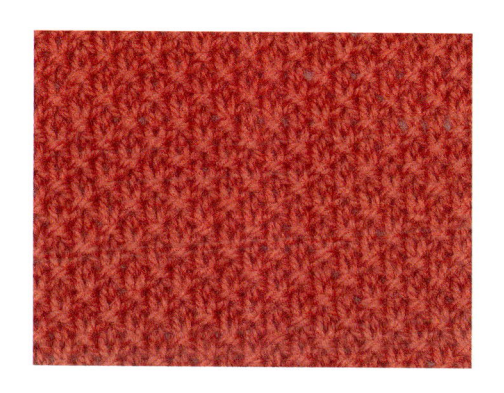

Moss Slip Stitch

Multiples: odd number pegs for flat and even number pegs for circular

To skip a peg, place the working yarn **behind** the next peg, leaving it unworked. Work the next peg keeping tension on the working yarn.

Since the fabric is stretched out while it's on the loom, it's important that the yarn floats are not loose.

Worked Flat

Row 1: K1, (skip 1, K1) across.

Row 2: P1, (skip 1, P1) across.

Row 3: K2, (skip 1, K1) across to last 3 pegs, skip 1, K2.

Row 4: P2, (skip 1, P1) across to last 3 pegs, skip 1, P2.

Repeat Rows 1-4 for pattern.

Worked Circular

Rnd 1: (Skip 1, K1) around.

Rnd 2: (Skip 1, P1) around.

Rnd 3: (K1, skip 1) around.

Rnd 4: (P1, skip 1) around.

Repeat Rnds 1-4 for pattern.

Roman Stitch

Multiple: any even number of pegs

Worked Flat

Rows 1-4: Knit across.

Rows 5 and 6: (K1, P1) across.

Repeat Rows 1-6 for pattern.

Worked Circular

Rnds 1-4: Knit around.

Rnd 5: (P1, K1) around.

Rnd 6: (K1, P1) around.

Repeat Rnds 1-6 for pattern.

Basket Stitch

Multiple: 6 pegs

Worked Flat and Circular

Row/Rnds 1 and 2: Knit across.

Row/Rnds 3-6: K1, P4, (K2, P4) across to last peg, K1.

Row/Rnds 7 and 8: Knit across.

Row/Rnds 9-12: P2, K2, (P4, K2) across to last 2 pegs, P2.

Repeat Rows/Rnds 1-12 for pattern.

Cornish Lattice

Multiples: 6 + 3 pegs for flat and 6 pegs for circular

Worked Flat

Row 1: P3, (K3, P3) across.

Row 2: Knit across.

Rows 3-5: Repeat Rows 1 and 2 once, then repeat Row 1 once **more**.

Rows 6-9: Knit across.

Row 10: K3, (P3, K3) across.

Row 11: Knit across.

Rows 12-14: Repeat Rows 10 and 11 once, then repeat Row 10 once **more**.

Rows 15-18: Knit across.

Repeat Rows 1-18 for pattern.

Worked Circular

Rnd 1: (P3, K3) around.

Rnd 2: Knit around.

Rnds 3-5: Repeat Rnds 1 and 2 once, then repeat Rnd 1 once **more**.

Rnds 6-9: Knit around.

Rnd 10: (K3, P3) around.

Rnd 11: Knit around.

Rnds 12-14: Repeat Rnds 10 and 11 once, then repeat Rnd 10 once **more**.

Rnds 15-18: Knit around.

Repeat Rnds 1-18 for pattern.

Seed Stitch Checks

Multiples: 10 + 5 pegs for flat and 10 pegs for circular

Worked Flat

Row 1: K5, ★ P1, (K1, P1) twice, K5; repeat from ★ across.

Row 2: K6, P1, K1, P1, ★ K7, P1, K1, P1; repeat from ★ across to last 6 pegs, K6.

Rows 3-5: Repeat Rows 1 and 2 once, then repeat Row 1 once **more**.

Row 6: P1, (K1, P1) twice, ★ K5, P1, (K1, P1) twice; repeat from ★ across.

Row 7: (K1, P1) twice, K7, ★ P1, K1, P1, K7; repeat from ★ across to last 4 pegs, (P1, K1) twice.

Rows 8-10: Repeat Rows 6 and 7 once, then repeat Row 6 once **more**.

Repeat Rows 1-10 for pattern.

Worked Circular

Rnd 1: ★ K5, P1, (K1, P1) twice; repeat from ★ around.

Rnd 2: K6, ★ P1, K1, P1, K7; repeat from ★ around to last 4 pegs, (P1, K1) twice.

Rnds 3-5: Repeat Rnds 1 and 2 once, then repeat Rnd 1 once **more**.

Rnd 6: ★ P1, (K1, P1) twice, K5; repeat from ★ around.

Rnd 7: (K1, P1) twice, ★ K7, P1, K1, P1; repeat from ★ around to last 6 pegs, K6.

Rnds 8-10: Repeat Rnds 6 and 7 once, then repeat Rnd 6 once **more**.

Repeat Rnds 1-10 for pattern.

Waffle Stitch

Multiples: 3 + 1 pegs for flat and 3 pegs for circular

Worked Flat

Rows 1-3: P1, (K2, P1) across.

Row 4: Purl across.

Repeat Rows 1-4 for pattern.

Worked Circular

Rnds 1-3: (P1, K2) around.

Rnd 4: Purl around.

Repeat Rnds 1-4 for pattern.

Diamond Brocade

Multiples: 8 + 1 pegs for flat and 8 pegs for circular

Worked Flat

Row 1: K4, P1, (K7, P1) across to last 4 pegs, K4.

Row 2: K3, P1, K1, P1, ★ K5, P1, K1, P1; repeat from ★ across to last 3 pegs, K3.

Row 3: K2, P1, (K3, P1) across to last 2 pegs, K2.

Row 4: K1, ★ P1, K5, P1, K1; repeat from ★ across.

Row 5: P1, (K7, P1) across.

Row 6: K1, ★ P1, K5, P1, K1; repeat from ★ across.

Row 7: K2, P1, (K3, P1) across to last 2 pegs, K2.

Row 8: K3, P1, K1, P1, ★ K5, P1, K1, P1; repeat from ★ across to last 3 pegs, K3.

Repeat Rows 1-8 for pattern.

Worked Circular

Rnd 1: K4, P1, (K7, P1) around to last 3 pegs, K3.

Rnd 2: K3, P1, K1, P1, ★ K5, P1, K1, P1; repeat from ★ around to last 2 pegs, K2.

Rnd 3: K2, P1, (K3, P1) around to last peg, K1.

Rnd 4: ★ K1, P1, K5, P1; repeat from ★ around.

Rnd 5: (P1, K7) around.

Rnd 6: ★ K1, P1, K5, P1; repeat from ★ around.

Rnd 7: K2, P1, (K3, P1) around to last peg, K1.

Rnd 8: K3, P1, K1, P1, ★ K5, P1, K1, P1; repeat from ★ around to last 2 pegs, K2.

Repeat Rnds 1-8 for pattern.

TWISTED STITCHES

BEGINNER

The e-wrap knit stitch produces a loose stitch which is good for using double strands of yarn or even a bulky or super bulky weight yarn.

The bottom strands of the e-wrap knit stitch cross each other, thus explaining why e-wrap knit stitches are called twisted stitches.

Loom knitters have a unique advantage when it comes to changing stitch gauge of twisted stitches. The size of the stitches can be changed by working variations of the twisted knit stitch. Choices are half stitch, double stitch, and triple stitch. Experiment and have fun!

25

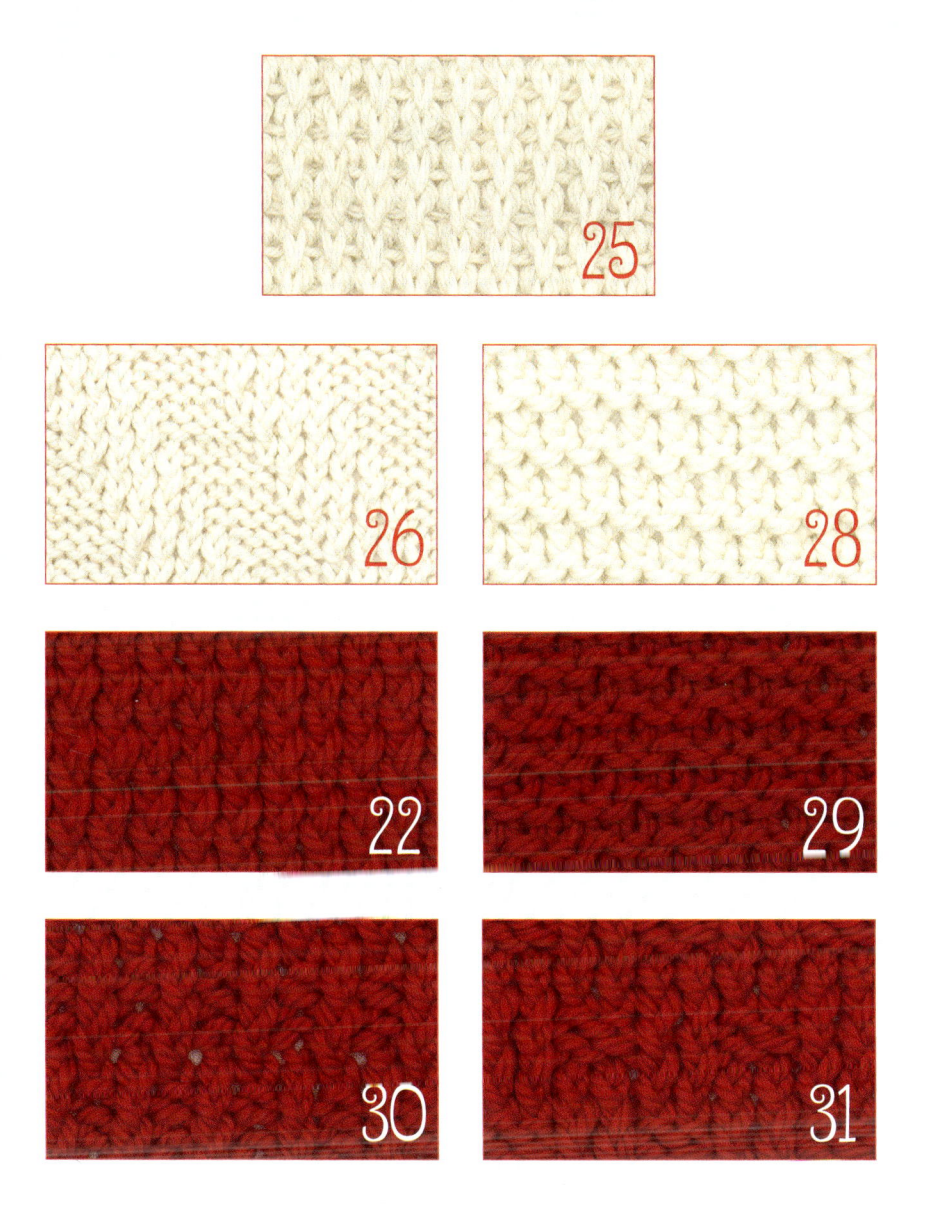

26 28

22 29

30 31

21

Twisted Stockinette

Multiple: any number of pegs

Worked Flat and Circular
E-wrap knit every row/rnd.

The reverse side of this stitch is called Reverse Twisted Stockinette Stitch. The purl stitches are also twisted.

Half Stitch

Multiple: any number of pegs

This stitch makes a thick fabric.

Worked Flat and Circular

Row/Rnd 1:

Step 1 - E-wrap 3 rows/rnds (in addition to the cast on row/rnd) without knitting the pegs. There will be 4 loops on each peg.

Step 2 - Using the tool, bring the 2 bottom loops over the top 2 loops and off the peg. There will be 2 loops on each peg.

Row/Rnd 2:

Step 1 - E-wrap 2 rows/rnds without knitting the pegs. There will be 4 loops on each peg.

Step 2 - Using the tool, bring the 2 bottom loops over the top 2 loops and off the peg. There will be 2 loops on each peg.

Repeat Row/Rnd 2 for pattern.

Double Stitch

Multiple: any number of pegs

This stitch is a tighter weave than the twisted stockinette stitch. Two strands form each stitch.

Worked Flat and Circular

Row/Rnd 1:

Step 1 - E-wrap 2 rows/rnds (in addition to the cast on row/rnd) without knitting the pegs. There will be 3 loops on each peg.

Step 2 - Using the tool, bring the bottom loop over the top 2 loops and off the peg. There will be 2 loops on each peg.

Row/Rnd 2:

Step 1 - E-wrap 1 row/rnd without knitting the pegs. There will be 3 loops on each peg.

Step 2 - Using the tool, bring the bottom loop over the top 2 loops and off the peg. There will be 2 loops on each peg.

Repeat Row/Rnd 2 for pattern.

Triple Stitch

Multiple: any number of pegs

Also known as Chunky Braid. A strand of yarn shows between the stitches, and the extra wraps add to each stitch, creating a different texture.

Worked Flat and Circular
Row/Rnd 1:
Step 1 - E-wrap 3 rows/rnds without knitting the pegs. There will be 4 loops on each peg.

Step 2 - Using the tool, bring the 3 bottom loops over the top loop and off the peg. There will be 1 loop on each peg.

Repeat Row/Rnd 1 for pattern.

Twisted Diagonal

Multiples: 8 + 2 pegs for flat and 8 pegs for circular

On the side facing you, the knit stitches will be twisted. On the opposite side, the purl stitches will be twisted.

Worked Flat

Row 1 (working from right to left)**:** (P4, EWK4) across to last 2 pegs, P2.

Row 2: P2, (EWK4, P4) across.

Row 3: EWK1, (P4, EWK4) across to last peg, P1.

Row 4: P1, (EWK4, P4) across to last peg, EWK1.

Row 5: EWK2, (P4, EWK4) across.

Row 6: (EWK4, P4) across to last 2 pegs, EWK2.

Rows 7 and 8: EWK3, P4, (EWK4, P4) across to last 3 pegs, EWK3.

Row 9: (EWK4, P4) across to last 2 pegs, EWK2.

Row 10: EWK2, (P4, EWK4) across.

Row 11: P1, (EWK4, P4) across to last peg, EWK1.

Row 12: EWK1, (P4, EWK4) across to last peg, P1.

Row 13: P2, (EWK4, P4) across.

Row 14: (P4, EWK4) across to last 2 pegs, P2.

Rows 15 and 16: P3, EWK4, (P4, EWK4) across to last 3 pegs, P3.

Repeat Rows 1-16 for pattern.

Worked Circular

Rnds 1 and 2 (working from left to right): (P4, EWK4) around.

Rnds 3 and 4: P3, EWK4, (P4, EWK4) around to last peg, P1.

Rnds 5 and 6: P2, EWK4, (P4, EWK4) around to last 2 pegs, P2.

Rnds 7 and 8: P1, EWK4, (P4, EWK4) around to last 3 pegs, P3.

Rnds 9 and 10: (EWK4, P4) around.

Rnds 11 and 12: EWK3, P4, (EWK4, P4) around to last peg, EWK1.

Rnds 13 and 14: EWK2, P4, (EWK4, P4) around to last 2 pegs, EWK2.

Rnds 15 and 16: EWK1, P4, (EWK4, P4) around to last 3 pegs, K3.

Repeat Rnds 1-16 for pattern.

Twisted Garter

Multiple: any number of pegs

Unlike Twisted Stockinette Stitch where every row has twisted stitches, only the knit rows are twisted.

Worked Flat and Circular

Row/Rnd 1: E-wrap knit across.

Row/Rnd 2: Purl across.

Repeat Rows/Rnds 1 and 2 for pattern.

Half Twisted Garter

Multiples: odd number of pegs for flat and an even number of pegs for circular

Worked Flat
Row 1: Purl across.

Row 2: K1, (EWK1, K1) across.

Row 3: Purl across.

Row 4: EWK1, (K1, EWK1) across.

Repeat Rows 1-4 for pattern.

Worked Circular
Rnd 1: Purl around.

Rnd 2: (EWK1, K1) around.

Rnd 3: Purl around.

Rnd 4: (K1, EWK1) around.

Repeat Rows 1-4 for pattern.

Twisted Check #1

Multiples: odd number of pegs for flat and an even number of pegs for circular

Worked Flat
Row 1: E-wrap knit across.

Rows 2-4: P1, (EWK1, P1) across.

Row 5: E-wrap knit across.

Rows 6-8: EWK1, (P1, EWK1) across.

Repeat Rows 1-8 for pattern.

Worked Circular
Rnd 1: E-wrap knit around.

Rnds 2-4: (EWK1, P1) around.

Rnd 5: E-wrap knit around.

Rnds 6-8: (P1, EWK1) around.

Repeat Rnds 1-8 for pattern.

Twisted Check #2

Multiples: 4 + 2 pegs for flat and 4 pegs for circular

Worked Flat

Rows 1 and 2: E-wrap knit across.

Rows 3 and 4: EWK2, (P2, EWK2) across.

Rows 5 and 6: E-wrap knit across.

Rows 7 and 8: P2, (EWK2, P2) across.

Repeat Rows 1-8 for pattern.

Worked Circular

Rnd 1 and 2: E-wrap knit around.

Rnds 3 and 4: (EWK2, P2) around.

Rnds 5 and 6: E-wrap knit around.

Rnds 7 and 8: (P2, EWK2) around.

Repeat Rnds 1-8 for pattern.

RIB PATTERNS

EASY

A Rib pattern is a combination of knit and purl stitches forming vertical ridges. It creates a stretchy fabric and is often worked at the bottom of sweaters, on cuffs, and around necklines. Knit 1, Purl 1 Rib is the most common ribbing. There are also many decorative rib patterns.

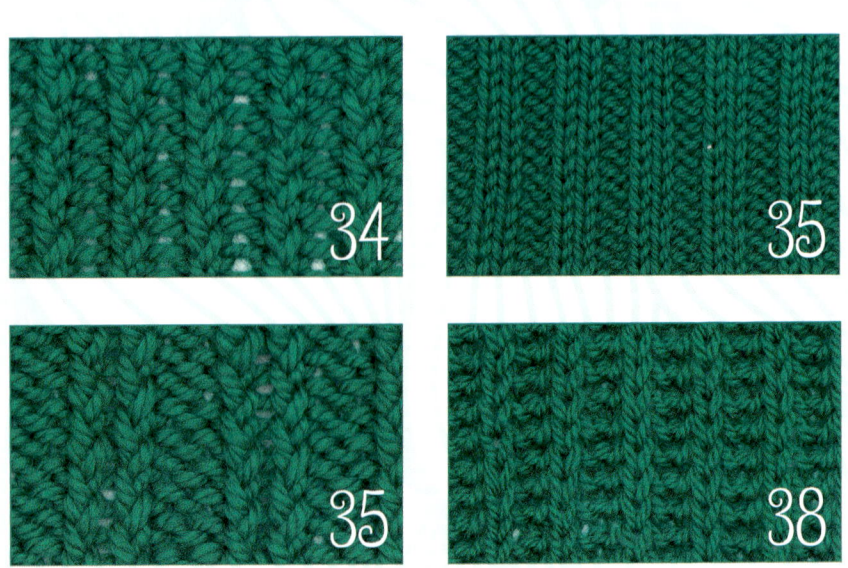

34

34

35

35

38

36

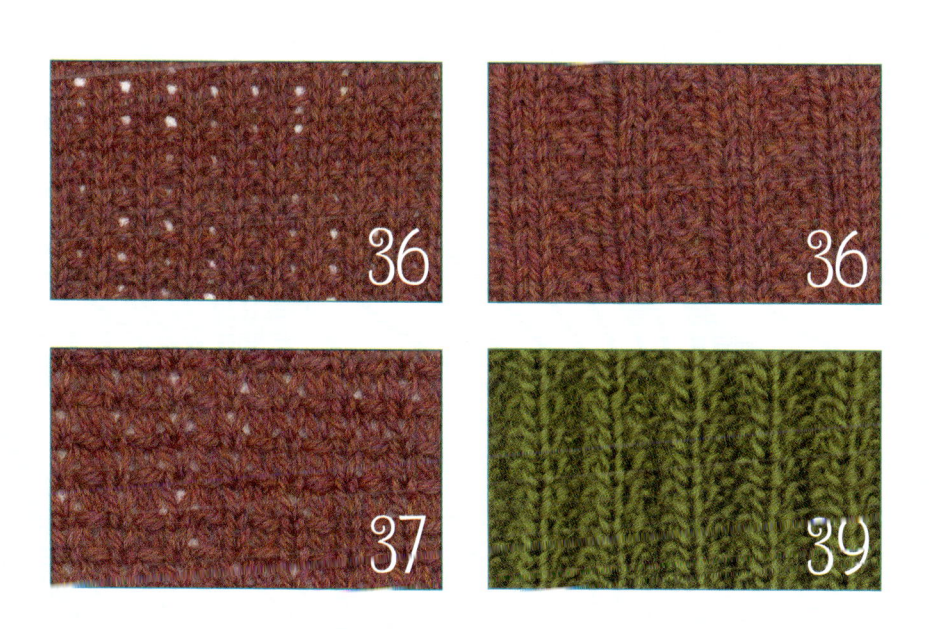

36

37

39

Knit 1, Purl 1 Rib

Multiple: any even number of pegs

Worked Flat

Row 1: (K1, P1) across.

Row 2: (P1, K1) across.

Repeat Rows 1 and 2 for pattern.

Worked Circular

Rnd 1: (K1, P1) around.

Repeat Rnd 1 for pattern.

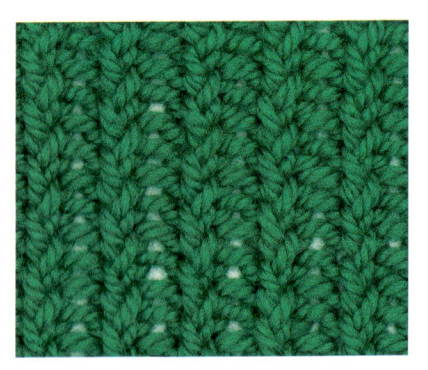

Twisted Knit 1, Purl 1 Rib

Multiple: any even number of pegs

Worked Flat

Row 1: (EWK1, P1) across.

Row 2: (P1, EWK1) across.

Repeat Rows 1 and 2 for pattern.

Worked Circular

Rnd 1: (EWK1, P1) around.

Repeat Rnd 1 for pattern.

Knit 2, Purl 2 Rib

Multiple: 4 pegs

Worked Flat

Row 1: (K2, P2) across.

Row 2: (P2, K2) across.

Repeat Rows 1 and 2 for pattern.

Worked Circular

Rnd 1: (K2, P2) around.

Repeat Rnd 1 for pattern.

Twisted Knit 2, Purl 2 Rib

Multiple: 4 pegs

Worked Flat

Row 1: (EWK2, P2) across.

Row 2: (P2, EWK2) across.

Repeat Rows 1 and 2 for pattern.

Worked Circular

Rnd 1: (EWK2, P2) around.

Repeat Rnd 1 for pattern.

Broken Rib

Multiples: any odd number of pegs for flat and any even number of pegs for circular

Worked Flat

Row 1: Knit across.

Row 2: K1, (P1, K1) across.

Repeat Rows 1 and 2 for pattern.

Worked Circular

Rnd 1: Knit around.

Rnd 2: (K1, P1) around.

Repeat Rnds 1 and 2 for pattern.

Double Garter Rib

Multiples: 4 + 2 pegs for flat and 4 pegs for circular

Worked Flat

Row 1: K2, (P2, K2) across.

Row 2: Knit across.

Repeat Rows 1 and 2 for pattern.

Worked Circular

Rnd 1: (K2, P2) around.

Rnd 2: Knit around.

Repeat Rnds 1 and 2 for pattern.

Slipped Rib

Multiples: any odd number of pegs for flat and any even number of pegs for circular

To skip 1 with yarn in front, use the tool to lift the loop from the next peg, bring the working yarn between the loop and the peg *(Fig. A)*, replace the loop.

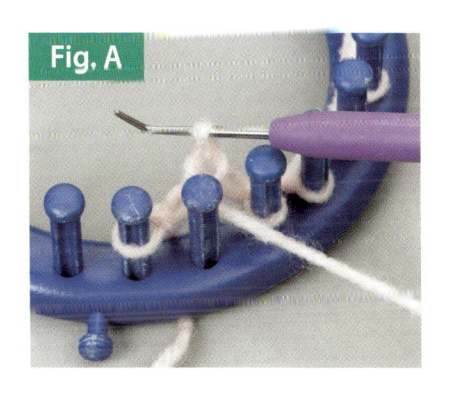

Fig. A

Worked Flat

Row 1: Knit across.

Row 2: K1, (skip 1 with yarn in front, K1) across.

Repeat Rows 1 and 2 for pattern.

Worked Circular

Rnd 1: Knit around.

Rnd 2: (Skip 1 with yarn in front, K1) around.

Repeat Rnds 1 and 2 for pattern.

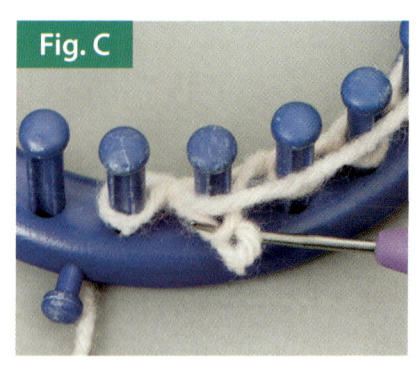

Fisherman's Rib

Multiple: any odd number of pegs for flat and any even number of pegs for circular

K1 below: Lift the loop from the next peg and place the stitch **below** it onto peg *(Fig. B)* along with the original loop (2 loops on peg), knit peg lifting both loops over the working yarn and off the peg *(Fig. C)*.

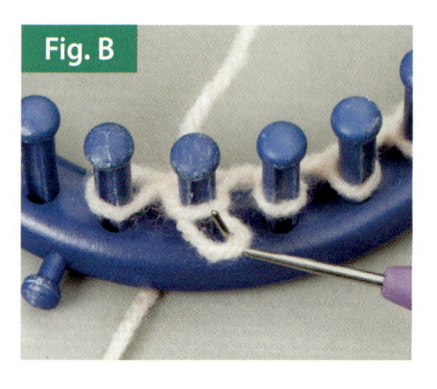

P1 below: Lift the loop from next peg and place the stitch **below** it onto peg along with the original loop (2 loops on peg), purl peg pulling the working yarn up through both loops.

Worked Flat
The first peg is skipped *(skip 1)* to create a finished look. Place the working yarn behind the peg to be skipped *(Fig. D)*.

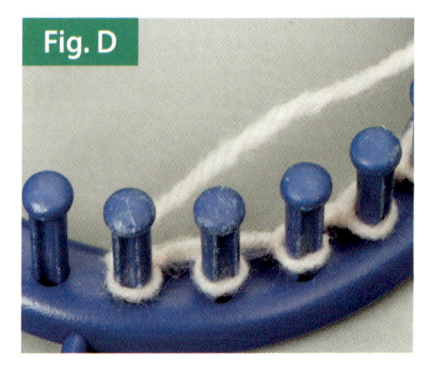

Row 1: Knit across.

Row 2: Skip 1, (K1 **below**, P1) across.

Row 3: Skip 1, K1, (P1 **below**, K1) across to last peg, P1.

Repeat Rows 2 and 3 for pattern.

Worked Circular
Rnd 1: Knit around.

Rnd 2: (K1 **below**, P1) around.

Rnd 3: (K1, P1 **below**) around.

Repeat Rnds 2 and 3 for pattern.

Moss Rib
Multiple: 4 + 1 pegs for flat and 4 pegs for circular

Worked Flat
Row 1: K2, P1, (K3, P1) across to last 2 pegs, K2.

Row 2: K1, (P3, K1) across.

Repeat Rows 1 and 2 for pattern.

Worked Circular
Rnd 1: K2, P1, (K3, P1) around to last peg, K1.

Rnd 2: (K1, P3) around.

Repeat Rnds 1 and 2 for pattern.

39

COLOR PATTERNS

EASY +

This collection of patterns will give you many options for adding color to your project. **Only one color is used on each row!** It only *looks* like two or more colors were used at a time. The colors are alternated every four rows for the Bargello Stitch and every two rows for the other pattern stitches.

Texture is added by using knit and purl stitches, forming garter ridges.

Yarn: You will need 3 colors for the Bargello Stitch and 2 colors for all of the other pattern stitches.

To create the color patterns in this section, you will learn two basic techniques: how to change colors *(page 42)* and how to skip a peg *(page 43)*.

46

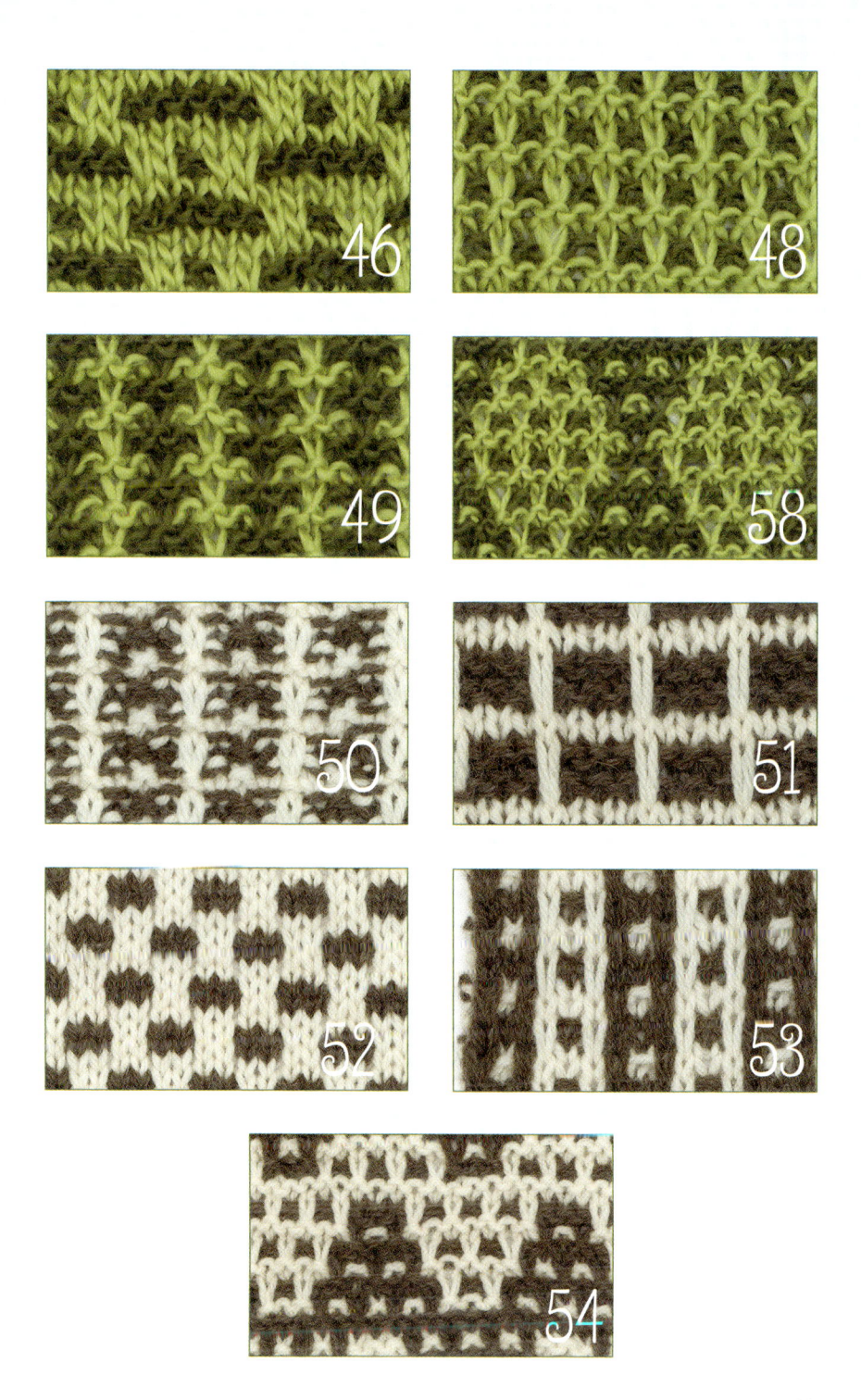

48

49

58

50

51

52

53

54

41

Changing Colors

The first time the second color is used, drop the color that you are using to the inside of the loom and begin working with the new color leaving a long end to weave in later.

To change colors at the end of a row or round, drop the color that you are working with to the inside of the loom. Then pick up the next color from underneath the strand *(Fig. A or B)*. This will twist the yarns.

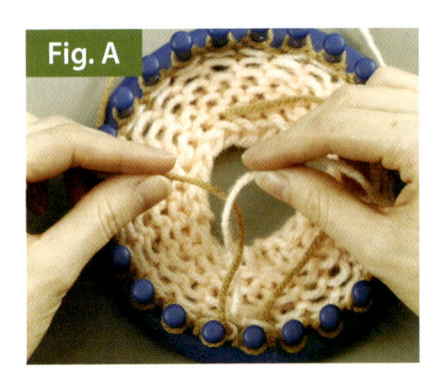

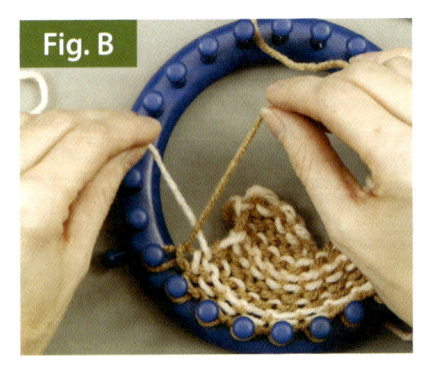

Fig. A

Fig. B

Do **not** cut the yarns until no longer needed; the unused yarn will be carried on the back of the fabric.

Skip a Peg

Skipping a peg allows the color from the previous row to be a part of the next colored row.

To skip a peg, place the working yarn **behind** the next peg, leaving it unworked *(Fig. C)*. Work the next peg keeping even tension on the working yarn.

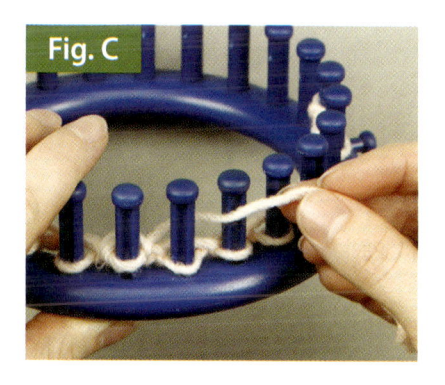

Fig. C

Since the fabric is stretched out while it's on the loom, it's important that the yarn floats behind the pegs are not loose.

Bargello Stitch

Multiples: 4 + 1 pegs for flat and 4 pegs for circular

With Color A, cast on from left to right.

Worked Flat

Rows 1 and 2: With Color A, knit across.

Alternate working 4 rows of each color. When skipping 3 pegs, hold yarn tightly behind the pegs to prevent loose stitches and strands.

Row 3: With Color B, K1, (skip 3, K1) across.

Row 4: K2, (skip 1, K3) across to last 3 pegs, skip 1, K2.

Rows 5 and 6: Knit across.

Rows 7-10: With Color C, repeat Rows 3-6.

Rows 11-14: With Color A, repeat Rows 3-6.

Repeat Rows 3-14 for pattern.

Worked Circular

Rnds 1 and 2: With Color A, knit around.

Begin alternating colors every 4 rnds.

Rnd 3: With Color B, (K1, skip 3) around.

Rnd 4: K2, (skip 1, K3) around to last 2 pegs, skip 1, K1.

Rnds 5 and 6: Knit around.

Rnds 7-10: With Color C, repeat Rnds 3-6.

Rnds 11-14: With Color A, repeat Rnds 3-6.

Repeat Rnds 3-14 for pattern.

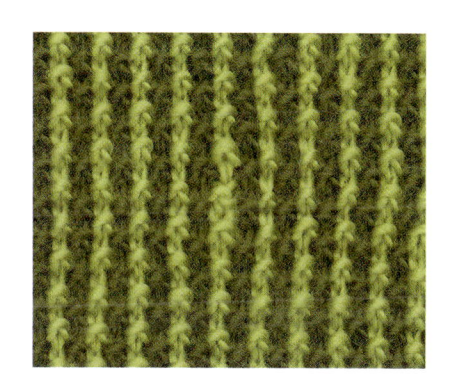

Colored Moss Stitch

Multiples: odd number of pegs for flat and an even number of pegs for circular

With Color A, cast on from left to right.

Worked Flat

Row 1: With Color A, K1, (skip 1, K1) across.

Row 2: P1, (skip 1, P1) across.

Row 3: With Color B, K2, (skip 1, K1) across to last 3 pegs, skip 1, K2.

Row 4: P2, (skip 1, P1) across to last 3 pegs, skip 1, P2.

Repeat Rows 1-4 for pattern.

Worked Circular
Rnd 1: With Color A, (skip 1, K1) around.

Rnd 2: (Skip 1, P1) around.

Rnd 3: With Color B, (K1, skip 1) around.

Rnd 4: (P1, skip 1) around.

Repeat Rnds 1-4 for pattern.

Dots & Dashes

Multiples: 10 + 7 pegs for flat and 10 pegs for circular

With Color A, cast on from left to right.

Worked Flat
Rows 1 and 2: With Color A, knit across.

Row 3: With Color B, K6, skip 2, K1, ★ skip 2, K5, skip 2, K1; repeat from ★ across to last 8 pegs, skip 2, K6.

46 www.leisurearts.com

Row 4: P6, skip 2, P1, ★ skip 2, P5, skip 2, P1; repeat from ★ across to last 8 pegs, skip 2, P6.

Rows 5 and 6: With Color A, knit across.

Row 7: With Color B, K1, skip 2, K1, ★ skip 2, K5, skip 2, K1; repeat from ★ across to last 3 pegs, skip 2, K1.

Row 8: P1, skip 2, P1, ★ skip 2, P5, skip 2, P1; repeat from ★ across to last 3 pegs, skip 2, P1.

Repeat Rows 1-8 for pattern.

Worked Circular

Rnds 1 and 2: With Color A, knit around.

Rnd 3: With Color B, ★ K5, skip 2, K1, skip 2; repeat from ★ around.

Rnd 4: ★ P5, skip 2, P1, skip 2; repeat from ★ around.

Rnds 5 and 6: With Color A, knit around.

Rnd 7: With Color B, ★ skip 2, K1, skip 2, K5; repeat from ★ around.

Rnd 8: ★ Skip 2, P1, skip 2, P5; repeat from ★ around.

Repeat Rnds 1-8 for pattern.

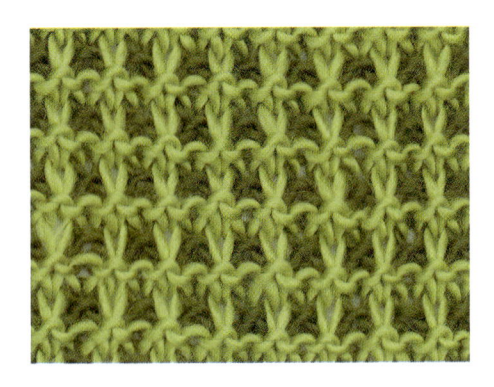

2-color Garter Stitch

Multiples: odd number of pegs for flat and an even number of pegs for circular

With Color A, cast on from left to right.

Worked Flat

Row 1: With Color A, knit across.

Row 2: Purl across.

Row 3: With Color B, K1, (skip 1, K1) across.

Row 4: With Color B, P1, (skip 1, P1) across.

Repeat Rows 1-4 for pattern.

Worked Circular

Rnd 1: With Color A, knit around.

Rnd 2: Purl around.

Rnd 3: With Color B, (skip 1, K1) around.

Rnd 4: With Color B, (skip 1, P1) around.

Repeat Rnds 1-4 for pattern.

Tweed Stitch

Multiples: 4 + 3 pegs for flat and 4 pegs for circular

With Color A, cast on from left to right.

Worked Flat
Row 1: With Color A, knit across.

Row 2: P1, (skip 1, P3) across to last 2 pegs, skip 1, P1.

Row 3: With Color B, K3, (skip 1, K3) across.

Row 4: P3, (skip 1, P3) across.

Row 5: With Color A, K1, (skip 1, K3) across to last 2 pegs, skip 1, K1.

Repeat Rows 2-5 for pattern.

Worked Circular
Rnd 1: With Color A, knit around.

Rnd 2: P1, (skip 1, P3) around to last 3 pegs, skip 1, P2.

Rnd 3: With Color B, (K3, skip 1) around.

Rnd 4: (P3, skip 1) around.

Rnd 5: With Color A, K1, (skip 1, K3) around to last 3 pegs, skip 1, K2.

Repeat Rnds 2-5 for pattern.

Colored Seed Stitch

Multiples: 4 + 3 pegs for flat and 4 pegs for circular

With Color A, cast on from left to right.

Worked Flat

Row 1: With Color A, P1, (K1, P1) across.

Row 2: K1, (P1, K1) across.

Row 3: With Color B, P1, K1, P1, ★ skip 1, P1, K1, P1; repeat from ★ across.

Row 4: K1, P1, K1, ★ skip 1, K1, P1, K1; repeat from ★ across.

Repeat Rows 1-4 for pattern.

Worked Circular

Rnd 1: With Color A, (K1, P1) around.

Rnd 2: (P1, K1) around.

Rnd 3: With Color B, ★ skip 1, P1, K1, P1; repeat from ★ around.

Rnd 4: ★ Skip 1, K1, P1, K1; repeat from ★ around.

Repeat Rnds 1-4 for pattern.

2-color Basket Stitch

Multiples: 4 + 3 pegs for flat and 4 pegs for circular

With Color A, cast on from left to right.

Worked Flat

Row 1: With Color A, knit across.

Row 2: With Color B, K3, (skip 1, K3) across.

Row 3: P3, (skip 1, P3) across.

Rows 4 and 5: Repeat Rows 2 and 3.

Rows 6 and 7: With Color A, knit across.

Repeat Rows 2-7 for pattern.

Worked Circular

Rnd 1: With Color A, knit around.

Rnd 2: With Color B, (skip 1, K3) around.

Rnd 3: (Skip 1, P3) around.

Rnds 4 and 5: Repeat Rnds 2 and 3.

Rnds 6 and 7: With Color A, knit around.

Repeat Rnds 2-7 for pattern.

2-stitch Check Stitch

Multiples: 4 pegs

With Color A, cast on from left to right.

Worked Flat

Rows 1 and 2: With Color A, knit across.

Rows 3 and 4: With Color B, K3, (skip 2, K2) across to last 5 pegs, skip 2, K3.

Rows 5 and 6: With Color A, knit across.

Rows 7 and 8: With Color B, K1, (skip 2, K2) across to last 3 pegs, skip 2, K1.

Repeat Rows 1-8 for pattern.

Worked Circular

Rnds 1 and 2: With Color A, knit around.

Rnds 3 and 4: With Color B, (skip 2, K2) around.

Rnds 5 and 6: With Color A, knit around.

Rnds 7 and 8: With Color B, (K2, skip 2) around.

Repeat Rnds 1-8 for pattern.

Dotted Ladder

Multiples: 6 + 5 pegs for flat and 6 pegs for circular

With Color A, cast on from left to right.

Worked Flat

Row 1: With Color B, knit across.

Row 2: With Color A, (K1, skip 1) twice, K3, ★ skip 1, K1, skip 1, K3; repeat from ★ across to last 4 pegs, (skip 1, K1) twice.

Row 3: K1, skip 1, P1, ★ skip 1, K3, skip 1, P1; repeat from ★ across to last 2 pegs, skip 1, K1.

Row 4: With Color B, K4, skip 1, K1, ★ skip 1, K3, skip 1, K1; repeat from ★ across to last 5 pegs, skip 1, K4.

Row 5: K4, skip 1, P1, ★ skip 1, K3, skip 1, P1; repeat from ★ across to last 5 pegs, skip 1, K4.

Repeat Rows 2-5 for pattern.

Worked Circular

Rnd 1: With Color B, knit around.

Rnd 2: With Color A, ★ skip 1, K1, skip 1, K3; repeat from ★ around.

Rnd 3: ★ Skip 1, P1, skip 1, K3; repeat from ★ around.

Rnd 4: With Color B, ★ K3, skip 1, K1, skip 1; repeat from ★ around.

Rnd 5: ★ K3, skip 1, P1, skip 1; repeat from ★ around.

Repeat Rnds 2-5 for pattern.

Chevron Mosaic

Multiples: 10 + 2 pegs for flat and 10 pegs for circular

With Color A, cast on from left to right.

Worked Flat

Row 1: With Color A, knit across.

Row 2: Purl across.

Beginning next row with Color B, alternate working 2 rows of each color.

Row 3: With next color, (K1, skip 1) twice, K3, ★ (skip 1, K1) 3 times, skip 1, K3; repeat from ★ across to last 5 pegs, skip 1, K1, skip 1, K2.

Row 4: P2, skip 1, P1, skip 1, P3, ★ (skip 1, P1) 3 times, skip 1, P3; repeat from ★ across to last 4 pegs, (skip 1, P1) twice.

Row 5: With next color, K4, skip 1, K1, ★ skip 1, K7, skip 1, K1; repeat from ★ across to last 6 pegs, skip 1, K5.

Row 6: P5, skip 1, P1, ★ skip 1, P7, skip 1, P1; repeat from ★ across to last 5 pegs, skip 1, P4.

Row 7: With next color, K2, skip 1, K5, ★ (skip 1, K1) twice, skip 1, K5; repeat from ★ across to last 4 pegs, (skip 1, K1) twice.

Row 8: (P1, skip 1) twice, P5, ★ (skip 1, P1) twice, skip 1, P5; repeat from ★ across to last 3 pegs, skip 1, P2.

Row 9: With next color, K3, (skip 1, K1) twice, ★ skip 1, K5, (skip 1, K1) twice; repeat from ★ across to last 5 pegs, skip 1, K4.

Row 10: P4, (skip 1, P1) twice, ★ skip 1, P5, (skip 1, P1) twice; repeat from ★ across to last 4 pegs, skip 1, P3.

Row 11: With next color, K1, skip 1, K7, ★ skip 1, K1, skip 1, K7; repeat from ★ across to last 3 pegs, skip 1, K2.

Row 12: P2, skip 1, P7, ★ skip 1, P1, skip 1, P7; repeat from ★ across to last 2 pegs, skip 1, P1.

Row 13: With next color, K2, ★ (skip 1, K1) 3 times, skip 1, K3; repeat from ★ across.

Row 14: ★ P3, (skip 1, P1) 3 times, skip 1; repeat from ★ across to last 2 pegs, P2.

Row 15: With next color, knit across.

Row 16: Purl across.

Repeat Rows 1-16 for pattern.

It takes 2 pattern repeats to form the chevron pattern.

Worked Circular

Rnd 1: With Color A, knit around.

Rnd 2: Purl around.

Beginning next rnd with Color B, alternate working 2 rnds of each color.

Rnd 3: With next color, (K1, skip 1) twice, K3, ★ (skip 1, K1) 3 times, skip 1, K3; repeat from ★ around to last 3 pegs, skip 1, K1, skip 1.

Rnd 4: (P1, skip 1) twice, P3, ★ (skip 1, P1) 3 times, skip 1, P3; repeat from ★ around to last 3 pegs, skip 1, P1, skip 1.

Rnd 5: With next color, K4, skip 1, K1, ★ skip 1, K7, skip 1, K1; repeat from ★ around to last 4 pegs, skip 1, K3.

Rnd 6: P4, skip 1, P1, ★ skip 1, P7, skip 1, P1; repeat from ★ around to last 4 pegs, skip 1, P3.

Rnd 7: With next color, skip 1, K1, skip 1, K5, ★ (skip 1, K1) twice, skip 1, K5; repeat from ★ across to last 2 pegs, skip 1, K1.

Rnd 8: Skip 1, P1, skip 1, P5, ★ (skip 1, P1) twice, skip 1, P5; repeat from ★ around to last 2 pegs, skip 1, P1.

Rnd 9: With next color, K3, (skip 1, K1) twice, ★ skip 1, K5, (skip 1, K1) twice; repeat from ★ around to last 3 pegs, skip 1, K2.

Rnd 10: P3, (skip 1, P1) twice, ★ skip 1, P5, (skip 1, P1) twice; repeat from ★ around to last 3 pegs, skip 1, P2.

Rnd 11: With next color, K1, skip 1, K7, ★ skip 1, K1, skip 1, K7; repeat from ★ around to last peg, skip 1.

Rnd 12: P1, skip 1, P7, ★ skip 1, P1, skip 1, P7; repeat from ★ around to last peg, skip 1.

Rnd 13: With next color, K2, ★ (skip 1, K1) 3 times, skip 1, K3; repeat from ★ around to last 8 pegs, (skip 1, K1) 4 times.

Rnd 14: P2, ★ (skip 1, P1) 3 times, skip 1, P3; repeat from ★ around to last 8 pegs, (skip 1, P1) 4 times.

Rnd 15: With next color, knit around.

Rnd 16: Purl around.

Repeat Rnds 1-16 for pattern.

It takes 2 pattern repeats to form the chevron pattern.

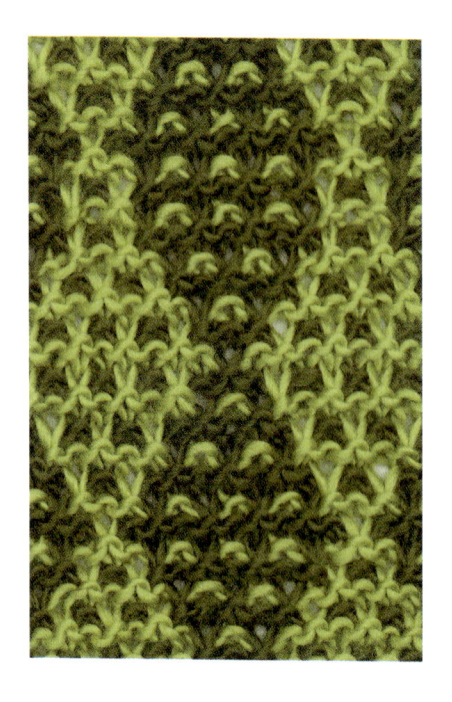

Harlequin Mosaic

Multiples: 10 + 3 pegs for flat and 10 pegs for circular

With Color B, cast on from left to right.

Worked Flat

Row 1: With Color A, K6, (skip 1, K9) across to last 7 pegs, skip 1, K6.

Row 2: P6, (skip 1, P9) across to last 7 pegs, skip 1, P6.

Row 3: With Color B, K2, skip 1, K1, skip 1, K3, ★ (skip 1, K1) 3 times, skip 1, K3; repeat from ★ across to last 5 pegs, skip 1, K1, skip 1, K2.

Row 4: P2, skip 1, P1, skip 1, P3, ★ (skip 1, P1) 3 times, skip 1, P3; repeat from ★ across to last 5 pegs, skip 1, P1, skip 1, P2.

Row 5: With Color A, K5, skip 1, K1, ★ skip 1, K7, skip 1, K1; repeat from ★ across to last 6 pegs, skip 1, K5.

Row 6: P5, skip 1, P1, ★ skip 1, P7, skip 1, P1; repeat from ★ across to last 6 pegs, skip 1, P5.

Row 7: With Color B, (K1, skip 1) twice, K5, (skip 1, K1) twice, ★ skip 1, K5, (skip 1, K1) twice; repeat from ★ across.

Row 8: (P1, skip 1) twice, P5, (skip 1, P1) twice, ★ skip 1, P5, (skip 1, P1) twice; repeat from ★ across.

Row 9: With Color A, K4, (skip 1, K1) twice, ★ skip 1, K5, (skip 1, K1) twice; repeat from ★ across to last 5 pegs, skip 1, K4.

Row 10: P4, (skip 1, P1) twice, ★ skip 1, P5, (skip 1, P1) twice; repeat from ★ across to last 5 pegs, skip 1, P4.

Row 11: With Color B, K2, skip 1, K7, ★ skip 1, K1, skip 1, K7; repeat from ★ across to last 3 pegs, skip 1, K2.

Row 12: P2, skip 1, P7, ★ skip 1, P1, skip 1, P7; repeat from ★ across to last 3 pegs, skip 1, P2.

Row 13: With Color A, K3, ★ (skip 1, K1) 3 times, skip 1, K3; repeat from ★ across.

Row 14: P3, ★ (skip 1, P1) 3 times, skip 1, P3; repeat from ★ across.

Row 15: With Color B, K1, (skip 1, K9) across to last 2 pegs, skip 1, K1.

Row 16: P1, (skip 1, P9) across to last 2 pegs, skip 1, P1.

Row 17: With Color A, K3, ★ (skip 1, K1) 3 times, skip 1, K3; repeat from ★ across.

Row 18: P3, ★ (skip 1, P1) 3 times, skip 1, P3; repeat from ★ across.

Row 19: With Color B, K2, skip 1, K7, ★ skip 1, K1, skip 1, K7; repeat from ★ across to last 3 pegs, skip 1, K2.

Row 20: P2, skip 1, P7, ★ skip 1, P1, skip 1, P7; repeat from ★ across to last 3 pegs, skip 1, P2.

Row 21: With Color A, K4, (skip 1, K1) twice, ★ skip 1, K5, (skip 1, K1) twice; repeat from ★ across to last 5 pegs, skip 1, K4.

Row 22: P4, (skip 1, P1) twice, ★ skip 1, P5, (skip 1, P1) twice; repeat from ★ across to last 5 pegs, skip 1, P4.

Row 23: With Color B, (K1, skip 1) twice, K5, (skip 1, K1) twice, ★ skip 1, K5, (skip 1, K1) twice; repeat from ★ across.

Row 24: (P1, skip 1) twice, P5, (skip 1, P1) twice, ★ skip 1, P5, (skip 1, P1) twice; repeat from ★ across.

Row 25: With Color A, K5, skip 1, K1, ★ skip 1, K7, skip 1, K1; repeat from ★ across to last 6 pegs, skip 1, K5.

Row 26: P5, skip 1, P1, ★ skip 1, P7, skip 1, P1; repeat from ★ across to last 6 pegs, skip 1, P5.

Row 27: With Color B, K2, skip 1, K1, skip 1, K3, ★ (skip 1, K1) 3 times, skip 1, K3; repeat from ★ across to last 5 pegs, skip 1, K1, skip 1, K2.

Row 28: P2, skip 1, P1, skip 1, P3, ★ (skip 1, P1) 3 times, skip 1, P3; repeat from ★ across to last 5 pegs, skip 1, P1, skip 1, P2.

Repeat Rows 1-28 for pattern.

Worked Circular
Rnd 1: With Color A, K5, (skip 1, K9) around to last 5 pegs, skip 1, K4.

Rnd 2: P5, (skip 1, P9) around to last 5 pegs, skip 1, P4.

Rnd 3: With Color B, (K1, skip 1) twice, K3, ★ (skip 1, K1) 3 times, skip 1, K3; repeat from ★ around to last 3 pegs, skip 1, K1, skip 1.

Rnd 4: (P1, skip 1) twice, P3, ★ (skip 1, P1) 3 times, skip 1, P3; repeat from ★ around to last 3 pegs, skip 1, P1, skip 1.

Rnd 5: With Color A, K4, skip 1, K1, ★ skip 1, K7, skip 1, K1; repeat from ★ around to last 4 pegs, skip 1, K3.

Rnd 6: P4, skip 1, P1, ★ skip 1, P7, skip 1, P1; repeat from ★ around to last 4 pegs, skip 1, P3.

Rnd 7: With Color B, skip 1, K1, skip 1, K5, ★ (skip 1, K1) twice, skip 1, K5; repeat from ★ around to last 2 pegs, skip 1, K1.

Rnd 8: Skip 1, P1, skip 1, P5, ★ (skip 1, P1) twice, skip 1, P5; repeat from ★ around to last 2 pegs, skip 1, P1.

Rnd 9: With Color A, K3, (skip 1, K1) twice, ★ skip 1, K5, (skip 1, K1) twice; repeat from ★ around to last 3 pegs, skip 1, K2.

Rnd 10: P3, (skip 1, P1) twice, ★ skip 1, P5, (skip 1, P1) twice; repeat from ★ around to last 3 pegs, skip 1, P2.

Rnd 11: With Color B, K1, skip 1, K7, ★ skip 1, K1, skip 1, K7; repeat from ★ around to last peg, skip 1.

Rnd 12: P1, skip 1, P7, ★ skip 1, P1, skip 1, P7; repeat from ★ around to last peg, skip 1.

Rnd 13: With Color A, K2, ★ (skip 1, K1) 3 times, skip 1, K3; repeat from ★ around to last 8 pegs, (skip 1, K1) 4 times.

Rnd 14: P2, ★ (skip 1, P1) 3 times, skip 1, P3; repeat from ★ around to last 8 pegs, (skip 1, P1) 4 times.

Rnd 15: With Color B, (skip 1, K9) around.

Rnd 16: (Skip 1, P9) around.

Rnd 17: With Color A, K2, ★ (skip 1, K1) 3 times, skip 1, K3; repeat from ★ around to last 8 pegs, (skip 1, K1) 4 times.

Rnd 18: P2, ★ (skip 1, P1) 3 times, skip 1, P3; repeat from ★ around to last 8 pegs, (skip 1, P1) 4 times.

Rnd 19: With Color B, K1, skip 1, K7, ★ skip 1, K1, skip 1, K7; repeat from ★ around to last peg, skip 1.

Rnd 20: P1, skip 1, P7, ★ skip 1, P1, skip 1, P7; repeat from ★ around to last peg, skip 1.

Rnd 21: With Color A, K3, (skip 1, K1) twice, ★ skip 1, K5, (skip 1, K1) twice; repeat from ★ around to last 3 pegs, skip 1, K2.

Rnd 22: P3, (skip 1, P1) twice, ★ skip 1, P5, (skip 1, P1) twice; repeat from ★ around to last 3 pegs, skip 1, P2.

Rnd 23: With Color B, skip 1, K1, skip 1, K5, ★ (skip 1, K1) twice, skip 1, K5; repeat from ★ around to last 2 pegs, skip 1, K1.

Rnd 24: Skip 1, P1, skip 1, P5, ★ (skip 1, P1) twice, skip 1, P5; repeat from ★ around to last 2 pegs, skip 1, P1.

Rnd 25: With Color A, K4, skip 1, K1, ★ skip 1, K7, skip 1, K1; repeat from ★ around to last 4 pegs, skip 1, K3.

Rnd 26: P4, skip 1, P1, ★ skip 1, P7, skip 1, P1; repeat from ★ around to last 4 pegs, skip 1, P3.

Rnd 27: With Color B, (K1, skip 1) twice, K3, ★ (skip 1, K1) 3 times, skip 1, K3; repeat from ★ around to last 3 pegs, skip 1, K1, skip 1.

Rnd 28: (P1, skip 1) twice, P3, ★ (skip 1, P1) 3 times, skip 1, P3; repeat from ★ around to last 3 pegs, skip 1, P1, skip 1.

Repeat Rnds 1-28 for pattern.

LACE PATTERNS

INTERMEDIATE

Lace knitting is formed by combining a decrease with an empty peg being e-wrapped *(known as yarn around peg, abbreviated YRP)*. The new loop is not worked until the next row or round, thus creating a hole in the fabric.

Lace rows are generally worked from left to right.

68

71

72

73

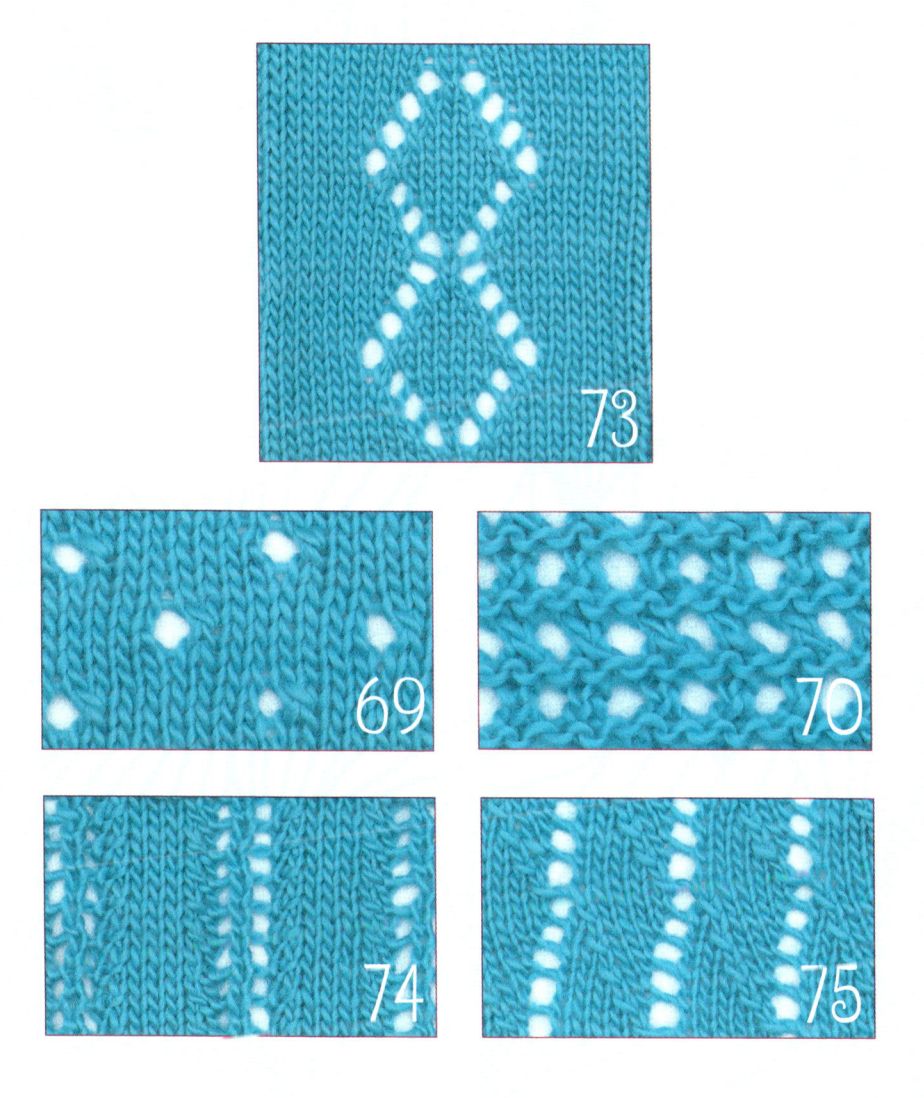

69

70

74

75

Decreases

LEFT DECREASE

Skip the next peg (peg B), and use the tool to move the loop from the next peg (peg A) to the **left** and place it on the skipped peg *(Fig. A)*. Knit the peg lifting the bottom 2 loops over the working yarn and off the peg.

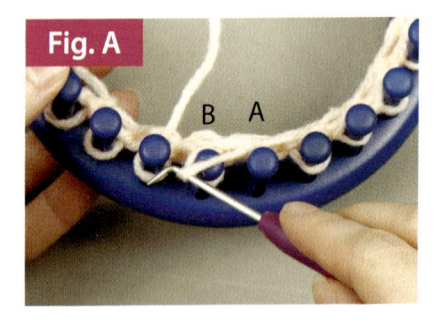

Fig. A

RIGHT DECREASE

Use the tool to move the loop on the next peg (peg B) to the **right** and place it on the next peg (peg A) *(Fig. B)*, knit the peg lifting the bottom 2 loops over the working yarn and off the peg.

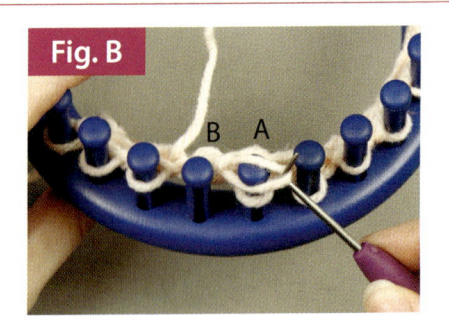

Fig. B

Yarn Around Peg
(abbreviated YRP)

E-wrap the empty peg clockwise *(Fig. C)*, when working a left to right row.

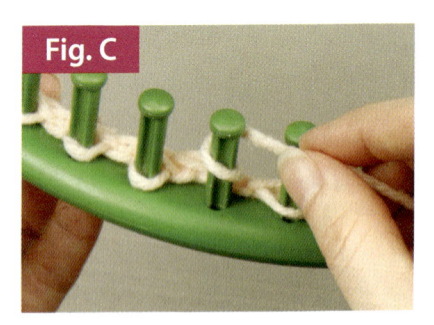

Fig. C

Combinations

If the YRP is worked before the decrease, the loop that will be part of the decrease needs to be moved in order to create an empty peg for the YRP.

YRP, LEFT DECREASE

Skip the next peg (peg B) and remove the loop from the next peg (peg A) using your fingers. Use the tool to move the loop from the skipped peg to the empty peg *(Fig. D)*, then place the loop you are holding on top of the loop you just moved. E-wrap the empty peg clockwise to create the YRP, and bring the yarn to the outside *(Fig. E)*. Knit the next peg (peg A) lifting the bottom 2 loops over the working yarn and off the peg (**left decrease made**).

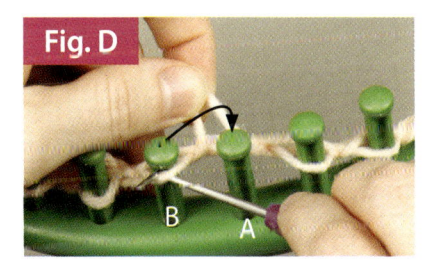

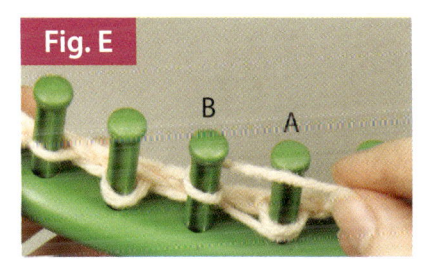

Fig. D

Fig. E

YRP, RIGHT DECREASE

Use the tool to move the loop from the next peg (peg B) to the peg on the **right** (peg A). E-wrap the empty peg clockwise to create the YRP, and bring the yarn to the outside *(Fig. F)*. Knit the next peg (peg A) lifting the bottom 2 loops over the working yarn and off the peg (**right decrease made**).

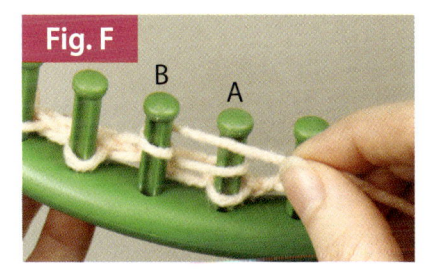

Fig. F

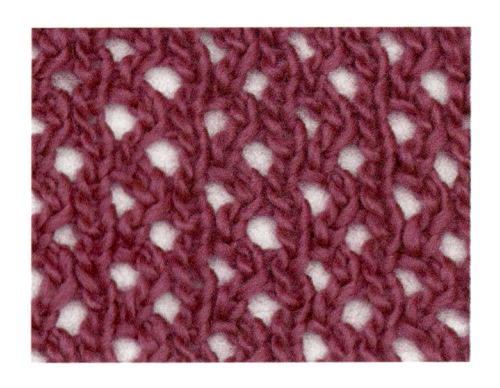

Easy Lace Stitch

Multiples: 3 + 1 pegs for flat and 3 pegs for circular

Worked Flat

Row 1 (working from right to left)**:** (K2, P1) across to last peg, K1.

Row 2: K1, ★ left decrease, YRP (e-wrap empty peg), K1; repeat from ★ across.

Row 3: K1, (P1, K2) across.

Row 4: K1, (YRP, left decrease, K1) across.

Repeat Rows 1-4 for pattern.

Worked Circular

Rnd 1 (working from left to right)**:** (P1, K2) around.

Rnd 2: ★ Left decrease, YRP (e-wrap empty peg), K1; repeat from ★ around.

Rnd 3: K1, P1, (K2, P1) around to last peg, K1.

Rnd 4: (YRP, left decrease, K1) around.

Repeat Rnds 1-4 for pattern.

Simple Eyelets

Multiple: 8 pegs

Worked Flat and Circular

Rows/Rnds 1-3: Knit across.

Row/Rnd 4 (working from left to right)**:** K1, YRP, left decrease, ★ K6, YRP, left decrease; repeat from ★ across to last 5 pegs, K5.

Rows/Rnds 5-7: Knit across.

Row/Rnd 8: K5, YRP, left decrease, (K6, YRP, left decrease) across to last peg, K1.

Row/Rnds 9-11: Knit across.

Repeat Rows/Rnds 4-11 for pattern.

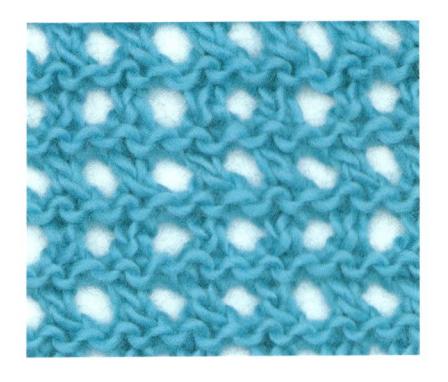

Ridged Lace Stitch

Multiples: odd number of pegs for flat and an even number of pegs for circular

Worked Flat

Row 1 (working from right to left)**:** Knit across.

Row 2: Purl across.

Row 3: Knit across.

Row 4: K1, (YRP, right decrease) across.

Row 5: Knit across.

Row 6: Purl across.

Row 7: Knit across.

Row 8: K1, (YRP, left decrease) across.

Repeat Rows 1-8 for pattern.

Worked Circular

Rnd 1 (working from left to right)**:** Knit around.

Rnd 2: Purl around.

Rnd 3: Knit around.

Rnd 4: (YRP, right decrease) around.

Rnd 5: Knit around.

Rnd 6: Purl around.

Rnd 7: Knit around.

Rnd 8: (YRP, left decrease) around.

Repeat Rnds 1-8 for pattern.

Lace Heart Panel

This pattern is worked across 13 pegs on a background of stockinette stitch. You can add any number of stitches before and after the panel to work either flat or circular.

Panel

Row 1 And All Odd Numbered Rows: Knit across.

Row 2 (working from left to right)**:** K5, left decrease, YRP (e-wrap empty peg), K6.

Row 4: K4, left decrease, YRP, K1, YRP, right decrease, K4.

Row 6: K3, left decrease, YRP, K3, YRP, right decrease, K3.

Row 8: K2, left decrease, YRP, K5, YRP, right decrease, K2.

Row 10: K1, left decrease, YRP, K7, YRP, right decrease, K1.

Row 12: Left decrease, YRP, K9, YRP, right decrease.

Row 14: Right decrease, move loop just made to the peg on the left, YRP, K3, left decrease, YRP, K4, YRP, left decrease.

Row 16: K2, YRP, right decrease, left decrease, YRP, K1, YRP, right decrease, left decrease, YRP, K2.

Repeat Rows 1-16 for pattern.

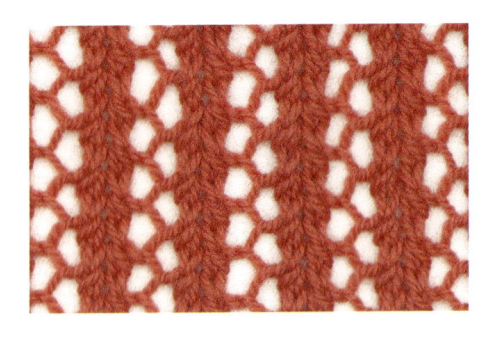

Faggoted Rib

Multiples: 4 + 2 pegs for flat and 4 pegs for circular

YRP, left decrease (working from right to left)**:** Move the loop from the next peg to the left, e-wrap empty peg, knit peg with 2 loops to complete left decrease.

Worked Flat

Row 1 (working from right to left)**:** K3, YRP, left decrease, ★ K2, YRP, left decrease; repeat from ★ across to last peg, K1.

Row 2: K3, YRP, right decrease, ★ K2, YRP, right decrease; repeat from ★ across to last peg, K1.

Repeat Rows 1 and 2 for pattern.

Worked Circular

Rnd 1 (working from left to right)**:** ★ K2, left decrease, YRP (e-wrap empty peg); repeat from ★ around.

Rnd 2: ★ YRP, right decrease, K2; repeat from ★ around.

Repeat Rnds 1 and 2 for pattern.

Row 2 (working from left to right)**:** K2, left decrease, YRP (e-wrap empty peg), K1, YRP, right decrease, K2.

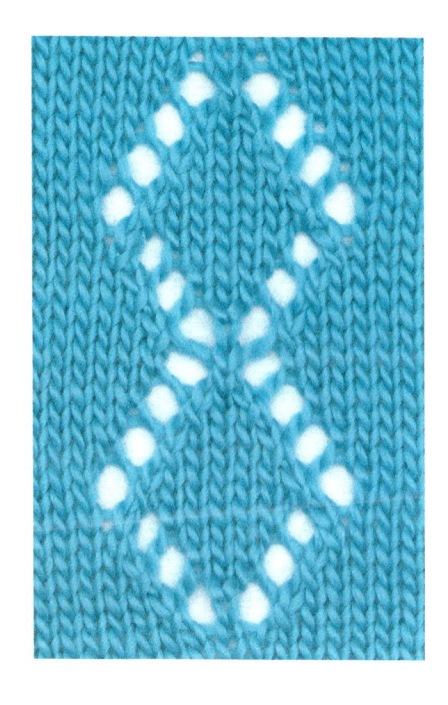

Row 4: K1, left decrease, YRP, K3, YRP, right decrease, K1.

Row 6: Left decrease, YRP, K5, YRP, right decrease.

Row 8: YRP, right decrease, K5, left decrease, YRP.

Diamond Lace Panel

This pattern is worked across 9 pegs on a background of stockinette stitch. You can add any number of stitches before and after the panel to work either flat or circular.

Row 10: K1, YRP, right decrease, K3, left decrease, YRP, K1.

Row 12: K2, YRP, right decrease, K1, left decrease, YRP, K2.

Row 14: K3, YRP, right decrease, move next loop to previous peg, bring bottom loop over loop and off the peg without knitting it, YRP, K3.

Repeat Rows 1-14 for pattern.

Panel
Row 1 And All Odd Numbered Rows: Knit across.

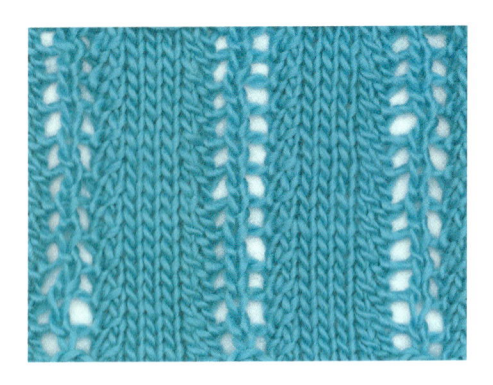

Millipedes Lace

Multiples: 10 + 1 pegs for flat and 10 pegs for circular

Worked Flat

Row 1 (working from right to left)**:** Knit across.

Row 2: K2, ★ † right decrease, move decrease and loop from next peg one at a time to an empty peg (creating a different empty peg), K1, YRP (e-wrap empty peg), K1, skip next 2 pegs and remove the loop from the next peg using your fingers. Use the tool to move the loop from the last skipped peg to the empty peg, then place the loop you are holding on top of the loop you just moved. Move the loop on the first skipped peg to the empty peg, YRP, K1, knit the next peg lifting the bottom 2 loops over the working yarn and off the peg **(left decrease made)** †, K3; repeat from ★ across to last 9 pegs, then repeat from † to † once, K2.

Repeat Rows 1 and 2 for pattern.

Worked Circular

Rnd 1 (working from left to right)**:** Knit across.

Rnd 2: ★ Right decrease, move decrease and loop from next peg one at a time to an empty peg (creating a different empty peg), K1, YRP (e-wrap empty peg), K1, skip next 2 pegs and remove the loop from the next peg using your fingers. Use the tool to move the loop from the last skipped peg to the empty peg, then place the loop you are holding on top of the loop you just moved. Move the loop on the first skipped peg to the empty peg, YRP, K1, knit the next peg lifting the bottom 2 loops over the working yarn and off the peg **(left decrease made)**, K3; repeat from ★ around.

Repeat Rnds 1 and 2 for pattern.

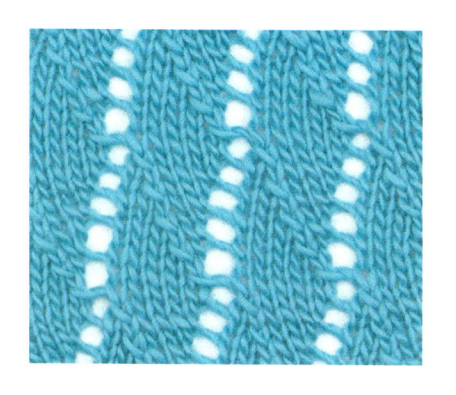

Overlapping Waves

Multiples: 6 + 5 pegs for flat and 6 pegs for circular

Worked Flat

Row 1 (working from right to left)**:** Knit across.

Row 2: K1, right decrease, move decrease just made to empty peg, YRP (e-wrap empty peg), ★ K4, right decrease, move decrease just made to empty peg, YRP; repeat from ★ across to last 2 pegs, K2.

Row 3: Knit across.

Row 4: K1, right decrease, move decrease to empty peg, YRP, ★ K3, right decrease, move decrease and loop from next peg one at a time to an empty peg (creating a different empty peg), K1, YRP; repeat from ★ across to last 2 pegs, K2.

Row 5: Knit across.

Row 6: K1, right decrease, move decrease to empty peg, YRP, K2, ★ right decrease, move decrease and loops from next 2 pegs one at a time to an empty peg, K2, YRP, K2; repeat from ★ across.

Row 7: Knit across.

Row 8: K1, right decrease, move decrease to empty peg, YRP, ★ K1, right decrease, move decrease and loops from next 3 pegs one at a time to an empty peg, K3, YRP; repeat from ★ across to last 2 pegs, K2.

Row 9: Knit across.

Row 10: K1, right decrease, move decrease to empty peg, YRP, ★ right decrease, move decrease and loops from next 4 pegs one at a time to an empty peg, K4, YRP; repeat from ★ across to last 2 pegs, K2.

Repeat Rows 1-10 for pattern.

Worked Circular

Rnd 1 (working from left to right)**:** Knit around.

Rnd 2: ★ K4, right decrease, move decrease just made to the empty peg, YRP (e-wrap empty peg); repeat from ★ around.

Rnd 3: Knit around.

Rnd 4: ★ K3, right decrease, move decrease and loop from next peg one at a time to an empty peg (creating a different empty peg), K1, YRP; repeat from ★ around.

Rnd 5: Knit around.

Rnd 6: ★ K2, right decrease, move decrease and loops from next 2 pegs one at a time to an empty peg, K2, YRP; repeat from ★ around.

Rnd 7: Knit around.

Rnd 8: ★ K1, right decrease, move decrease and loops from next 3 pegs one at a time to an empty peg, K3, YRP; repeat from ★ around.

Rnd 9: Knit around.

Rnd 10: ★ Right decrease, move decrease and loops from next 4 pegs one at a time to an empty peg, K4, YRP; repeat from ★ around.

Repeat Rnds 1-10 for pattern

CABLES

INTERMEDIATE

There are many variations of cable patterns, but all are based on switching the position of stitches on the pegs. The direction in which the top stitches lean depends on how the stitches are crossed.

Each panel includes two purl stitches on each side of the cable pattern to help the cable show up. The Honeycomb pattern is an allover pattern made up of many cables.

One panel can be added to a project or many panels can be worked to create a pattern stitch.

All the cable instructions in this section are given for flat knitting, but they will also work inserted in a circular piece following the same instructions.

Additional Supplies: You will need a cable needle for all cables except for the Mock Cable.

The easiest Cable patterns are given first.

79

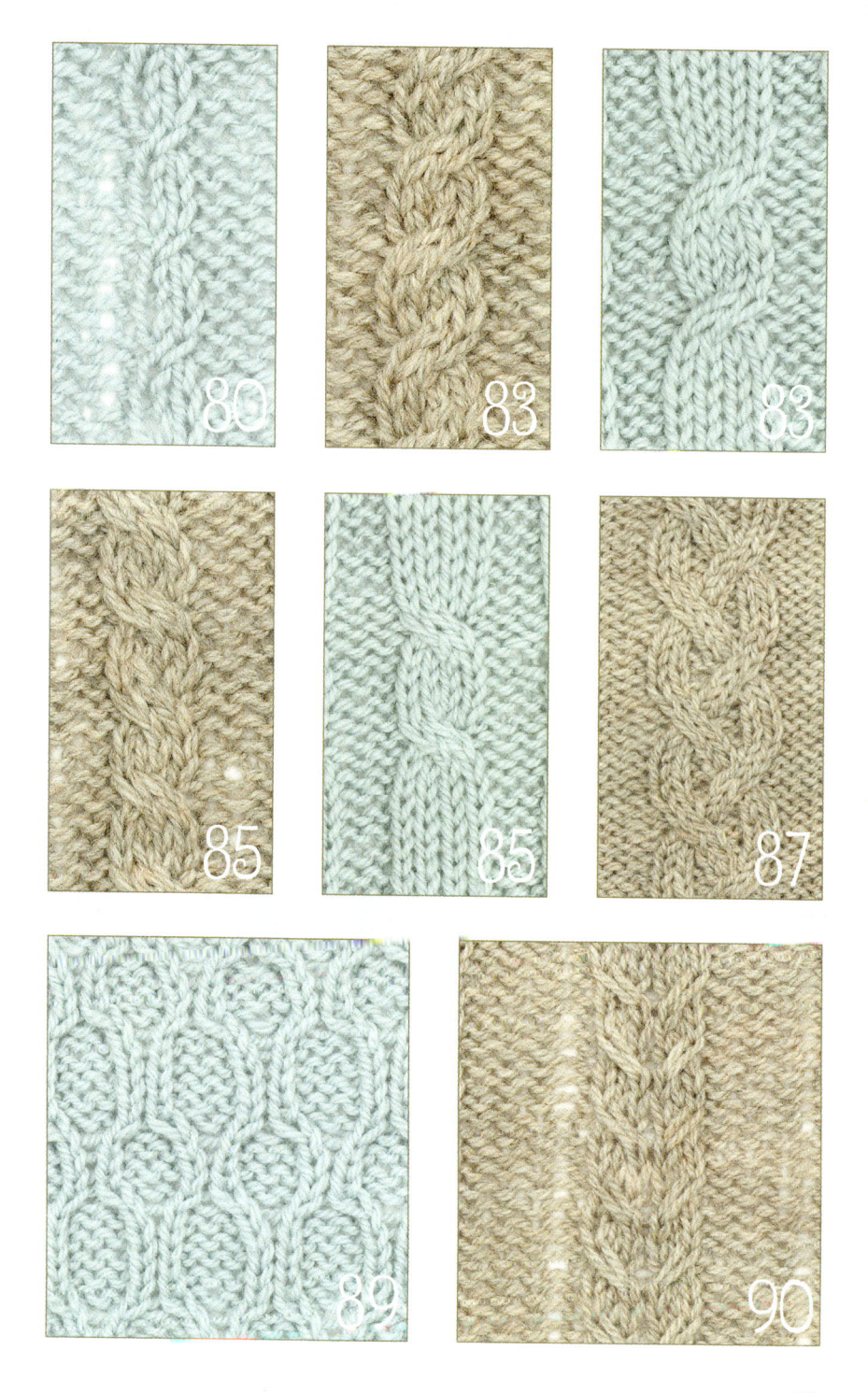

Mock Cable

This is a simple 2 stitch cable that is easy to make.

Panel: Worked across 6 pegs.

Worked Flat
Rows 1-3: P2, K2, P2.

Row 4 (working from left to right)**:** P2, bring the working yarn behind the next peg, then back to the outside and knit the next peg. Bring the working yarn to the inside of the loom, remove the loop just made using your fingers. Use the tool to move the loop from the skipped peg to the empty peg *(Fig. A)*, then place the loop you are holding on the new empty peg, bring the yarn between the pegs and knit that peg, P2.

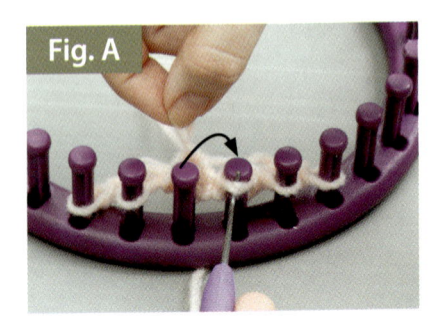

Repeat Rows 1-4 for pattern.

CROSS 4 RIGHT

(abbreviated C4R)

(uses 4 pegs)

Bring the working yarn behind the next 2 pegs, then back to the outside *(Fig. B)*.

Fig. B

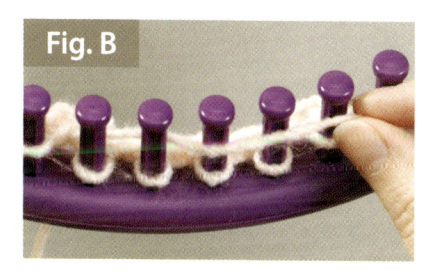

Knit the next 2 pegs, then place them onto a cable needle *(Fig. C)* and let it hang at the inside of the loom.

Fig. C

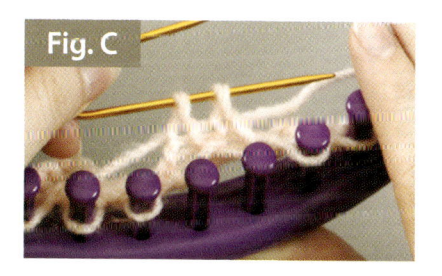

Bring the working yarn behind all 4 pegs, then back to the outside before the first skipped peg *(Fig. D)*.

Fig. D

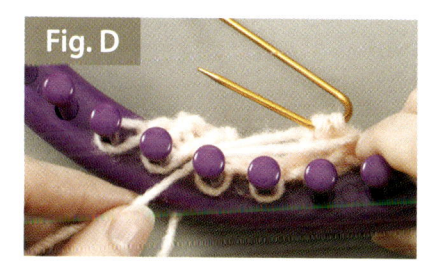

Knit the 2 skipped pegs, then use the tool to move them to the empty pegs, keeping them in the same order *(Fig. E)*.

Fig. E

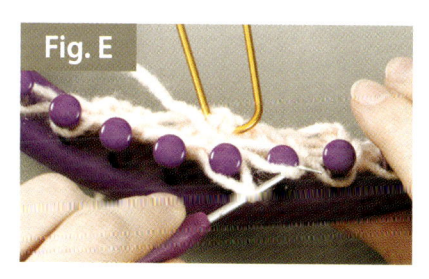

Place the loops from the cable needle onto the new empty pegs, keeping them in the same order *(Fig. F)*.

Fig. F

TIP:

The stitches should always be worked **loosely**, allowing them to be easily moved. Once the cable stitches have been moved, take up the slack of each stitch by gently tugging on the yarn.

Right 4 Stitch Cable

This cable uses the Cross 4 Right *(Figs. B-F, pages 81 & 82)*.

Panel: Worked across 8 pegs.

Worked Flat

Rows 1-3: P2, K4, P2.

Row 4 (working from left to right)**:** P2, C4R, P2.

Repeat Rows 1-4 for pattern.

Right Eccentric Cable

Panel: Worked across 8 pegs.

Worked Flat

Rows 1-3: P2, K4, P2.

Row 4 (working from left to right)**:** P2, C4R, P2.

Rows 5-9: P2, K4, P2.

Row 10: P2, C4R, P2.

Rows 11-21: P2, K4, P2.

Repeat Rows 4-21 for pattern.

CROSS 4 LEFT

(abbreviated C4L)

(uses 4 pegs)

Place the loops from the next 2 pegs onto a cable needle and let it hang at the inside of the loom. Bring the working yarn behind the 2 empty pegs, then back to the outside *(Fig. G)*.

Fig. G

Knit the next 2 pegs, then use the tool to move them to the empty pegs, keeping them in the same order *(Fig. H)*. With the working yarn outside the loom, place the loops from the cable needle onto the new empty pegs, keeping them in the same order and knit them. Take up the slack of each stitch by gently tugging on the yarn.

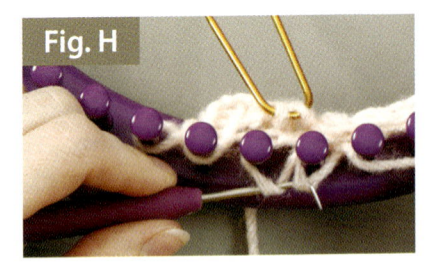

Fig. H

Left 4 Stitch Cable

This cable uses the Cross 4 Left *(Figs. G & H, page 84)*.

Panel: Worked across 8 pegs.

Worked Flat
Rows 1-3: P2, K4, P2.

Row 4 (working from left to right): P2, C4L, P2.

Repeat Rows 1-4 for pattern.

Left Eccentric Cable

Panel: Worked across 8 pegs.

Worked Flat
Rows 1-3: P2, K4, P2.

Row 4 (working from left to right): P2, C4L, P2.

Rows 5-9: P2, K4, P2.

Row 10: P2, C4L, P2.

Rows 11-21: P2, K4, P2.

Repeat Rows 4-21 for pattern.

TWIST 3 LEFT

(abbreviated T3L)

(uses 3 pegs)

Place the loop from the next peg onto a cable needle and let it hang at the inside of the loom. Bring the working yarn behind the empty peg and then back to the outside *(Fig. I)* and knit the next 2 pegs, then move them one at a time to the empty pegs, keeping them in the same order. Place the stitch from the cable needle onto the new empty peg and purl it.

Fig. I

TWIST 3 RIGHT

(abbreviated T3R)

(uses 3 pegs)

Bring the working yarn behind the next 2 pegs, then back to the outside and purl the next peg. Place it onto a cable needle and let it hang at the inside of the loom. Bring the working yarn behind all 3 pegs, then back to the outside before the skipped pegs *(Fig. J)*. Knit the 2 skipped pegs, then use the tool to move them one at a time to the empty pegs, keeping them in the same order. Place the stitch from the cable needle onto the empty peg.

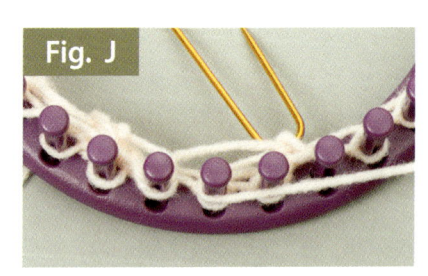

Fig. J

Braided Cable

This cable is a combination of cables: Cross 4 Right *(Figs. B-F, pages 81 & 82)*, Cross 4 Left *(Figs. G & H, page 84)*, Twist 3 Left *(Fig. I, page 86)*, and Twist 3 Right *(Fig. J, page 86)*.

Panel: Worked across 13 pegs.

Worked Flat

Row 1 (working from right to left)**:** P2, K2, P2, K4, P3.

Row 2: P2, T3L, T3R, T3L, P2.

Row 3: P3, K4, P2, K2, P2.

Row 4: P2, K2, P2, C4R, P3.

Row 5: P3, K4, P2, K2, P2.

Row 6: P2, T3R, T3L, T3R, P2.

Row 7: P2, K2, P2, K4, P3.

Row 8: P3, C4L, P2, K2, P2.

Repeat Rows 1-8 for pattern.

Worked Circular

Rnd 1 (working from left to right)**:** P3, K4, P2, K2, P2.

Rnd 2: P2, T3L, T3R, T3L, P2.

Rnd 3: P2, K2, P2, K4, P3.

Rnd 4: P2, K2, P2, C4R, P3.

Rnd 5: P2, K2, P2, K4, P3.

Rnd 6: P2, T3R, T3L, T3R, P2.

Rnd 7: P3, K4, P2, K2, P2.

Rnd 8: P3, C4L, P2, K2, P2.

Repeat Rnds 1-8 for pattern.

LEFT PURL CROSS
(abbreviated LPC)
(uses 3 pegs)

Place the stitches from the next 2 pegs onto a cable needle and let it hang at the inside of the loom. Bring the working yarn behind the empty pegs and then back to the outside and knit the next peg, then move it to the first empty peg *(Fig. K)*. Place the stitches from the cable needle onto the empty pegs, keeping them in the same order and purl them.

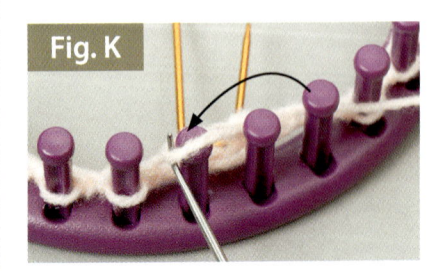

Fig. K

RIGHT PURL CROSS
(abbreviated RPC)
(uses 3 pegs)

Bring the working yarn behind the next peg, then back to the outside and purl the next 2 pegs. Place them onto a cable needle and let it hang at the inside of the loom. Bring the working yarn behind all 3 pegs, then back to the outside before the skipped peg. Knit the skipped peg, then use the tool to move it to the second empty peg *(Fig. L)*. Place the stitches from the cable needle onto the empty pegs, keeping them in the same order.

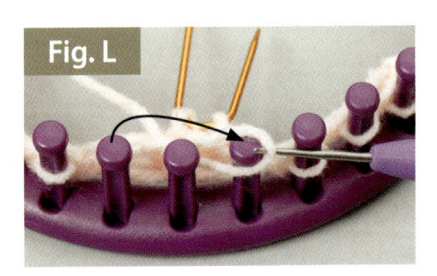

Fig. L

Honeycomb Cable

This cable uses the Left and Right Purl Cross *(Figs. K & L, page 88)*.

Multiple: 6 + 4 pegs for flat and 6 pegs for circular

Worked Flat

Rows 1-3: K2, P2, K2, (P4, K2) across to last 4 pegs, P2, K2.

Row 4 (working from left to right)**:** K2, (LPC, RPC) across to last 2 pegs, K2.

Rows 5-7: K3, P4, (K2, P4) across to last 3 pegs, K3.

Row 8: K2, (RPC, LPC) across to last 2 pegs, K2.

Repeat Rows 1-8 for pattern.

Worked Circular

Rnds 1-3 (working from left to right)**:** P2, K2, (P4, K2) around to last 2 pegs, P2.

Rnd 4: (LPC, RPC) around.

Rnds 5-7: K1, P4, (K2, P4) around to last peg, K1.

Rnd 8: (RPC, LPC) around.

Repeat Rnds 1-8 for pattern.

Gull Stitch

Panel: Worked across 10 pegs.

Worked Flat

Row 1: P2, K6, P2.

Row 2 (working from left to right)**:** P2, K2, skip 2 pegs with yarn in **back** *(Fig. C, page 43)*, K2, P2.

Row 3: P2, K2, skip 2 pegs with yarn in **back**, K2, P2.

Row 4: P2, place the loops from the next 2 pegs onto a cable needle and let it hang at the inside of the loom. Bring the working yarn behind the 2 empty pegs and then back to the outside and knit the next peg, then move it to the first empty peg.
Place the loops from the cable needle onto the empty pegs, keeping them in the same order and knit them **(left cross made)**.
Bring the working yarn behind the next peg, then back to the outside and knit the next 2 pegs. Place them onto a cable needle and let it hang at the inside of the loom. Bring the working yarn behind all 3 pegs, then back to the outside before the skipped peg. Knit the skipped peg, then use the tool to move it to the second empty peg. Place the loops from the cable needle onto the empty pegs, keeping them in the same order **(right cross made)**, P2.

Repeat Rows 1-4 for pattern.

GENERAL INSTRUCTIONS

Abbreviations

C4L	cross 4 left
C4R	cross 4 right
EWK	e-wrap knit
K	knit
LPC	left purl cross
P	purl
Rnd(s)	Round(s)
RPC	right purl cross
T3L	twist 3 left
T3R	twist 3 right
YRP	yarn around peg

Symbols & Terms

★ — work instructions following ★ as many **more** times as indicated in addition to the first time.

† to † — work all instructions from first † to second † as **many** times as specified.

( ) or [ ] — work enclosed instructions **as many** times as specified by the number immediately following **or** contains explanatory remarks.

colon (:) — the number(s) given after a colon at the end of a row or round denote(s) the number of pegs you should have occupied at the end of that row or round.

working yarn — the strand coming from the skein.

Yarn Weight Symbol & Names	SUPER FINE 1	FINE 2	LIGHT 3	MEDIUM 4	BULKY 5	SUPER BULKY 6
Type of Yarns in Category	Sock, Fingering, Baby	Sport, Baby	DK, Light Worsted	Worsted, Afghan, Aran	Chunky, Craft, Rug	Bulky, Roving

E-wrap Cast On

The yarn can be anchored before beginning as follows: Make a slip knot leaving a 6" (15 cm) end and insert it in the center of the loom from top to bottom and place it on the side peg, pulling the strand to tighten the loop. Remove the anchor after working 2 or 3 rows or rounds.

Wrap the working yarn around the first peg in a **clockwise** direction, ending at the inside of the loom and behind the next peg *(Fig. 1a)*.

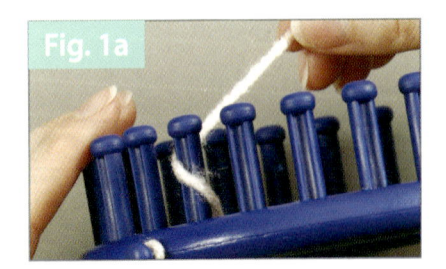

Fig. 1a

Moving around the loom **counter-clockwise** and wrapping each peg with the same tension, wrap the next peg **clockwise**, ending at the inside of the loom and behind the next peg *(Fig. 1b)*.

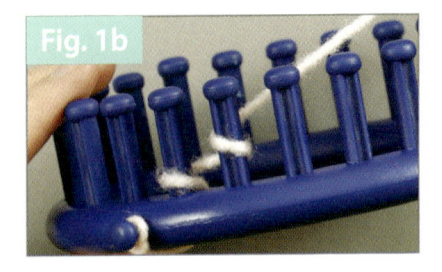

Fig. 1b

Continue around the loom, pushing the loops down with your other hand as you go, until all of the pegs have been wrapped for projects that are worked circularly, ending at the inside of the loom *(Fig. 1c)*. For projects that are worked as flat knitting without using all of the pegs, only wrap as many pegs as specified for the project that you are making.

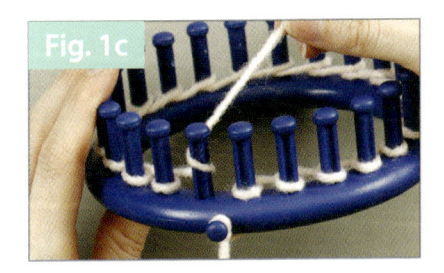

Fig. 1c

Knit Stitch
(abbreviated K)

Step 1: Loosely lay the working yarn on the outside of the loom, **above** the loops that are already on the pegs *(Fig. 2a)*.

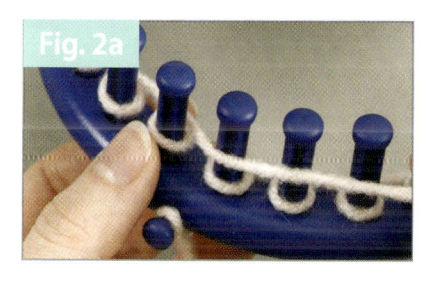

Fig. 2a

Step 2: Using the tool, lift the bottom loop over the working yarn and off the peg *(Fig. 2b)*, allowing a new stitch to form around the peg *(Fig. 2c)*. Push the new loop down with your other hand.

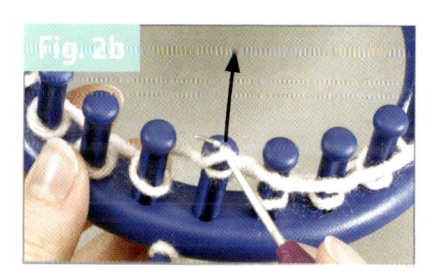

Fig. 2b

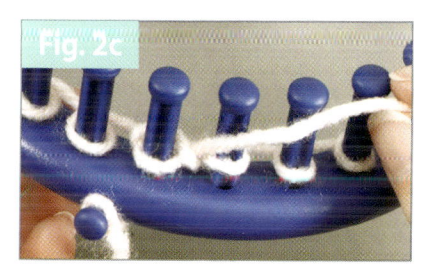

Fig. 2c

Repeat Steps 1 and 2 for each peg to be knitted.

TIP:
The working yarn should wrap around the peg as it forms a stitch. The stitches will form naturally if you gently push the back of the previous stitches down as you work.

E-wrap Knit Stitch
(abbreviated EWK)

WORKING CIRCULAR
When working circularly (making a tubular project), always work around the loom **counter-clockwise** wrapping the pegs in the same direction as the e-wrap cast on.

Step 1: Wrap the next peg **clockwise** *(Fig. 3a)*. There will be 2 loops on the peg.

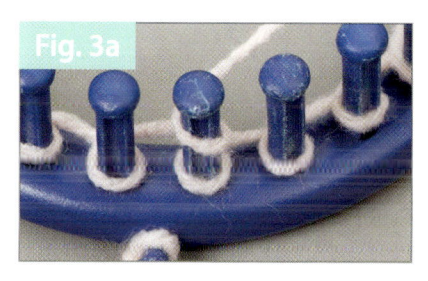

Fig. 3a

93

Step 2: Using the tool, lift the bottom loop over the top loop and off the peg *(Fig. 3b)*, completing the e-wrap knit stitch.

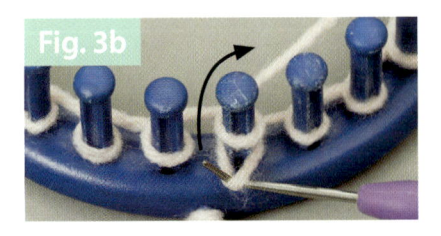

Fig. 3b

Repeat Steps 1 and 2 for each e-wrap knit stitch.

If all of the pegs in a round are to be e-wrapped knit, you can wrap all of the pegs at the same time (Step 1), then complete the stitches (Step 2).

WORKING FLAT
When working flat (back and forth in rows), the pegs are wrapped in the opposite direction on each row. The yarn should always cross at the inside edge of the loom while leaving a loop on the outside of each peg.

On a Left to Right Row
Work same as for Circular knitting *(Figs. 3a & b, pages 93 and 94)*.

On a Right to Left Row
Step 1: Wrap the next peg **counter clockwise** *(Fig. 3c)*. There will be 2 loops on the peg.

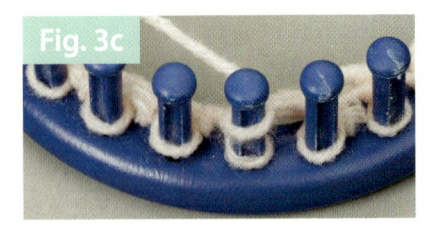

Fig. 3c

Step 2: Using the tool, lift the bottom loop over the top loop and off the peg *(Fig. 3d)*, completing the e-wrap knit stitch.

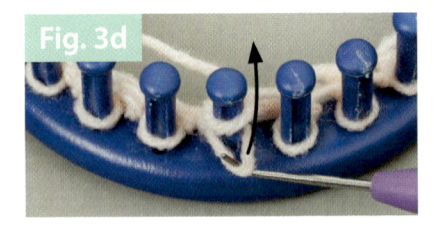

Fig. 3d

Repeat Steps 1 and 2 for each e-wrap knit stitch.

If the first peg of a row is e-wrap knit following the last peg of the previous row being e-wrap knit, the first peg is wrapped in the same direction as the last stitch on the previous row. The remaining pegs are wrapped in the opposite direction as the first peg.

Purl Stitch
(abbreviated P)

Step 1: Lay the working yarn on the outside of the loom, **below** the loops on the pegs *(Fig. 4a)*.

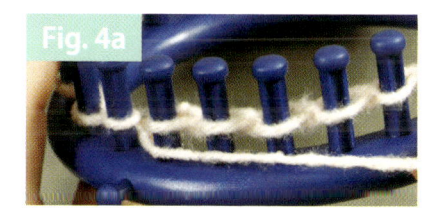

Fig. 4a

Step 2: Insert the tool down through the loop on the peg (from top to bottom) *(Fig. 4b)*.

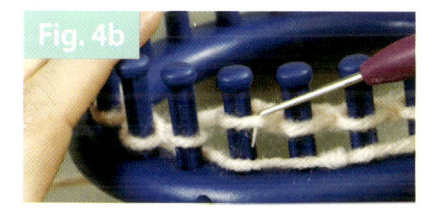

Fig. 4b

Step 3: With the tip of the tool over the working yarn, turn the tool as you pull the working yarn up through the loop on the peg forming a new loop *(Fig. 4c)*.

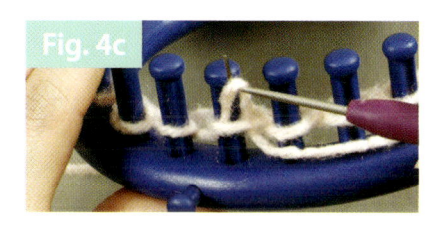

Fig. 4c

Step 4: Using your fingers, lift the original loop off the peg. Place the newly formed loop onto the empty peg *(Fig. 4d)*. Tighten the loop by gently pulling the working yarn, allowing the stitch to curve around the outside half of the peg.

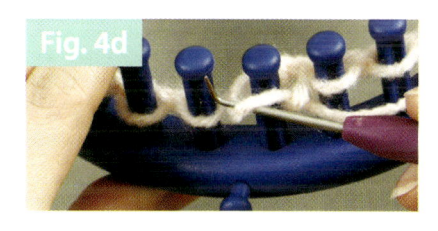

Fig. 4d

Repeat Steps 1-4 for each peg to be purled.

Simple Bind Off

Step 1: Knit or e-wrap knit 2 pegs.

Step 2: Use the tool to remove the loop from the peg just worked and place it on the first peg, leaving the second peg empty *(Fig. 5a)*. Lift the bottom loop over the top loop and off the peg *(Fig. 5b)*.

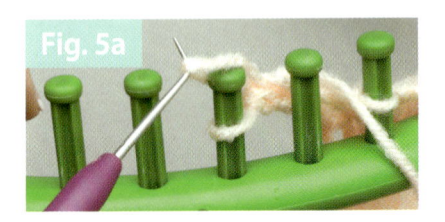

Fig. 5a

Fig. 5b

Step 3: Move the loop from the first peg to the second peg.

Step 4: Knit or e-wrap knit the next peg.

To bind off all stitches, repeat Steps 2-4 until 2 loops remain, then repeat Step 2 once **more**.

Cut the yarn and pull the end through the final loop.

96 www.leisurearts.com